D1637132

ST

The Bobby Orr Story

An engaging account of his rise to fame as the brightest star in pro hockey

The Bobby Orr Story

by John Devaney
Illustrated with photographs
Random House   New York

PHOTOGRAPH CREDITS: Canada Wide—Pictorial Parade, 23, 38, 55, 126 top
right and top left, 149; Vincent Claps-Movement Associates, 6; Kevin Fitzgerald—
SPORT Magazine, 71, back endpaper; Ken Regan—Camera 5, 1, 2, 10, 20; United
Press International, front endpapers, 21 top and bottom, 22, 40, 56 top, 56–57
bottom, 57 top, 72–73, 73 bottom, 74 bottom, 92–93, 94 top, 95, 96, 97 top, 98 bottom,
110 top and bottom, 111, 125, 127 top, 126–127 bottom, 136–137 top, 136–137 bottom,
138 top; Wide World Photos, 39, 70 left and right, 74 top, 92 top, 94 bottom, 97 bottom,
98 top, 136 top, 137 top, 138 bottom.

Cover: SPORTS ILLUSTRATED photo by Neil Leifer © Time Inc.

Library of Congress Cataloging in Publication Data
Devaney, John.   The Bobby Orr story.   (Pro hockey library)
SUMMARY: A biography of the Boston Bruins' star defenseman considered by many
to be one of the best all-round hockey players of all time.
1. Orr, Bobby, 1948-   —Juvenile literature.
[1. Orr, Bobby, 1948-   2. Hockey—Biography]   I. Title.
GV848.5.O7D48 1973   796.9′62′0924   [B] [92]   73-6661
ISBN 0-394-82612-4   ISBN 0-394-92612-9 (lib. bdg.)

For John and Gene

One draws from many streams to put together a book on Bobby Orr. I am especially indebted to Herb Ralby of the Bruins and John Halligan of the Rangers for material. The book Bobby Orr and the Big, Bad Bruins, *by Stan Fischler, is invaluable for any one who wants to know more about Bobby and his teammates. Magazine and newspaper articles by Leo Monahan, Red Fisher, Jack Olsen, Mark Mulvoy, Tom Fitzgerald, Herbert Warren Wind, Trent Frayne, Bill Surface, Chris Lydon and Pete Axthelm were also of considerable help.*

J.D.

CONTENTS

The Bobby Orr Story

The Greatest of Them All

The puck slithered across the ice. The New York Rangers' Jim Dorey stopped the black rubber disc on the blade of his stick. He swiveled on his skates and saw another Ranger cutting toward the Boston Bruin goal. Dorey flicked the puck toward his teammate, but the Bruins' Mike Walton veered into its path and caught it on his stick.

Bruin defenseman Bobby Orr was speeding toward the blue line and Walton pushed the puck toward him. His blond hair flying, Orr took the puck and streaked down the ice toward the Ranger goal.

Two Ranger defensemen, Dorey and Brad Park, zigzagged backward to help goaltender Ed Giacomin protect the net. The New York crowd let out a surprised roar as Orr somehow accelerated again, like a racing car bursting into high gear.

He flew between the two defensemen before they could close the gap and skidded to a stop in front of the goal mouth, ice flying off the blades of his skates. He faked to the left with his stick, then right. Goalie Giacomin lunged to the right, and Bobby flipped the puck into the left corner of the cage.

Goal!

Orr had scored. The Bruins led 1–0 in this fourth game of the finals of the 1971–72 Stanley Cup finals.

The Ranger fans settled back into their seats, murmuring disappointment, while a small knot of Boston fans cheered. Bruins were smacking Bobby on his padded legs with their sticks. He cruised in small circles, staring at the ice, a delighted smile on his face.

Pie McKenzie, a Bruin forward, sidled up to him. "Even a race horse couldn't have caught you when you flew between those defensemen," Pie said. Bobby laughed.

His shift ended, Bobby skated quickly to the bench. He sat down, watching the action. Trainer Dan Canney glanced at Orr. Canney knew that Bobby's left knee was swollen and throbbing with pain. Twice the doctors had operated on that knee. They'd have to operate again in a few weeks.

Bobby shouldn't even be playing. He couldn't make his turns and pivots the way he usually did—yet he was still the most sensational skater on the ice. Despite the pain, he wanted to help

win the Bruins' second Stanley Cup in three
years.

A few minutes later he had to leave the bench
and go to the clubhouse. There Canney strapped
fresh ice packs on the knee to reduce the swelling.
Then Bobby returned to the bench. He gripped
the knee, feeling the coldness of the ice pack
under his stockings. Sweat trickled down his
long-jawed, fair face. Sometimes, when he stood
up quickly, pain made him wince. But he didn't
want the pain to show. The coach might see it. He
wanted all of his ice time.

The coach, Tom Johnson, gave him a signal.
Bobby and his partner on defense, curly-haired
Dallas Smith, leaped over the boards and onto the
ice. The puck was behind the Ranger cage. He
skated toward "the point"—a spot on the blue
line where defensemen station themselves when
their team is attacking. From "the point" a
defenseman can keep the puck from slithering
toward his team's goal. And if he gets possession
he can slam a long 40-foot shot toward the
opposing goal or pass to a teammate near the
goal.

At "the point" Bobby saw teammate Johnny
"Chief" Bucyk collect the puck behind the
Ranger net. Suddenly Bobby left "the point" and
sped for the Ranger goal, leaving the Bruin goal
unprotected behind him. If a Ranger picked up
the puck, he would have a clear shot toward the
Bruin goal.

Bucyk saw Bobby dart from "the point." He

passed the puck to Pie McKenzie, who whisked the puck across the ice into Bobby's path. Bobby swatted at the puck like a batter swinging at an ankle-high fastball. There was a loud *clack!* as the stick hit rubber. The puck flew through a welter of legs and Ranger goaltender Ed Giacomin dove—too late. The puck flew past him and into the nets.

Goal! Number two for Bobby in this game. The Bruins led, 2–0.

Early in the second period the Bruins still held that thin 2–0 lead. Shortly after he came on ice for his shift, Bruin winger Don Marcotte intercepted a Ranger pass and scooted up the left board, shuttling the puck in front of him. Bobby took off after him, again boldly leaving his side of the ice wide open.

Sensing that Orr was behind him, Marcotte raised his stick and dropped the puck in front of Bobby's skates. Then he barged in front of the Ranger goal, trying to obscure goaltender Giacomin's view.

Bobby raised his stick to let fly the shot. Giacomin tensed, straining to follow that black rubber. Marcotte, who had skidded to a stop near the corner of the cage, turned and looked for the shot. He saw the puck streaking right on to his stick. It was a perfect pass from Bobby.

Giacomin had gone after the shot that never came. Now he tried to turn to defend against Marcotte, but he was too late. Marcotte back-handed the puck into the cage as casually as a man flipping away a match.

The Bruins were ahead 3–0, and Bobby Orr had two goals and an assist. Now Boston concentrated on protecting its lead. Bobby hung back, throwing his 6-foot, 185-pound body into 210-pound forwards, checking them against the boards. When Rangers rushed up the ice with the puck, his stick was as quick as a serpent's tongue, stealing away the puck.

Between periods the trainer worked on his puffed knee. Bobby worried that it might lock or collapse under him. That had happened before. He couldn't go on playing much longer, the knee hurt so bad.

The Rangers fought back and scored twice. They fought with their fists, too, and once Bobby and Brad Park traded punches to the jaw.

Once the Bruins lost a skater, who had been sent to the penalty box for tripping a Ranger. The Bruins won the face-off and flipped the puck to Bobby. He hugged the puck to his stick and skated in circles with a line of Rangers chasing after him. They tried to knock the puck away, but he held on to it. They tried to knock him down, but he stayed on his feet. For 30 seconds of the two-minute penalty Bobby skated in circles with the puck, "killing" the penalty. Finally three Rangers cornered him. He shot the puck the length of the rink, and by the time the Rangers recovered it and organized an attack, the penalty time was nearly ended. The Rangers did not score.

The Bruins won, 3–2. They led now in this best-of-seven Stanley Cup finals, three games to one.

The Bruins trooped wearily into their clubhouse. Derek "Turk" Sanderson looked at a reporter. "Sooner or later," Turk said, "Orr's genius wins games like this for us."

In the Ranger clubhouse Brad Park shook his head, sadness etched on his round face. "And Orr played hurt," he was saying to another Ranger. "I'd like to hurt as bad as he did and play that well."

A reporter asked Ranger coach Emile Francis why the Rangers had failed to score when the Bruins were short one man. Francis stared sadly at the reporters. "With Orr," he said in a soft voice, "the Bruins are never short-handed."

Most hockey fans agree: Bobby Orr is the greatest all-around hockey player of all time.

Some Gordie Howe fans may disagree and Bobby Hull fans may say no. A few other all-time greats may also have their supporters. But one thing is indisputable: Bobby Orr can do more things on a hockey rink than any man in history.

There are only two basic things you must do in a hockey game: you must block the puck from going into your goal, you must knock the puck into the opposing goal. As a defenseman Bobby blocked so many pucks that teammate Phil Esposito claimed the Bruin goaltenders should pay Orr half their salary. At the same time Bobby knocked so many pucks into opposing goals that one year he led the National Hockey League in scoring— and no other defenseman has ever done that before or since.

"He can block the shots," said Montreal's great Jean Beliveau. "He can skate. He can shoot. Is there anything more?"

"Bobby has a shot as accurate and as hard as most any forward in this league," goaltender Cesare Maniago once said.

"Most defensemen can't do much with the puck when they take it away from you, and that's why they're playing defense," said NHL veteran Phil Goyette. "But Orr handles the puck well enough to be a forward and if he gets a chance to shoot he's extremely accurate."

Bobby's accomplishments are the equivalent to those of a baseball pitcher who wins 30 games *and* leads the league in hitting with a .350 average. He played both ends of the ice—attacking the enemy goal like a forward, then racing back to protect his own goal as a defenseman. "I see him make a fantastic play shooting at our goal," said Ranger coach Emile Francis, "and when we skate back up the ice, there he is to meet us. You rarely catch him out of position."

To play both ends takes endurance. Skating up and down a 200-foot-long rink at full speed for a whole game is like running a 100-yard dash over and over again—maybe 20 or 25 times a night.

And to be a double-threat defenseman, Orr needed enough speed to win most of the "dashes" too. "Most pro hockey players come down on you at one speed and then turn on a burst," defenseman Bob Plager once said. "But Orr can break into a third speed and then turn into a fourth. You just can't keep up with him." "You holler at him for loafing," said one of Bobby's coaches. "Then you see he is passing everybody." Frank "King" Clancy, who had seen every great hockey player in 50 years, confirmed what other less experienced fans were saying. Although he had watched such legendary stars as Morenz, Shore, Richard, Beliveau, Hull and Howe, he said, "Bobby Orr is the best player his age I have ever seen."

Bobby Orr came into the National Hockey League at the age of eighteen. Already he was considered the greatest young hockey star in history. The Boston Bruin management was counting on him to make winners out of a losing team, and before he put a skate on NHL ice, Bobby was the third-highest-paid player in the game. The pressure on the young man was tremendous. Fans watched his every move, expecting miracles.

Some players resented him and his high salary. They punched him, shoved him, kicked him, tripped him. Hockey writers pointed out his mistakes—even minor things that would have gone unnoticed in another player. He had to be great—or else.

What kind of man was he and what did the pressure do to him? Did he succeed?

To understand how Bobby Orr got to be the person he is, you drive some 150 miles north from Toronto in Canada to the small resort town of Parry Sound which is perched on the edge of Georgian Bay, a part of Lake Huron. There the Orr family has lived for three generations and most of the family remains to this day. Bobby's grandfather came to Parry Sound from Ireland. Bobby's father was a promising hockey player who decided to stay in Parry Sound and Bobby's brothers and sisters still live nearby. It was here in the frozen winters and sun-splashed summers that hockey's top star grew up.

HOCKEY'S BIGGEST STAR

Bobby waits for a face-off (right), helps Bruin goalie Ed Johnston fend off a scoring threat (top, far right), and bulls his way past Rangers Arnie Brown and Brad Park (bottom, far right).

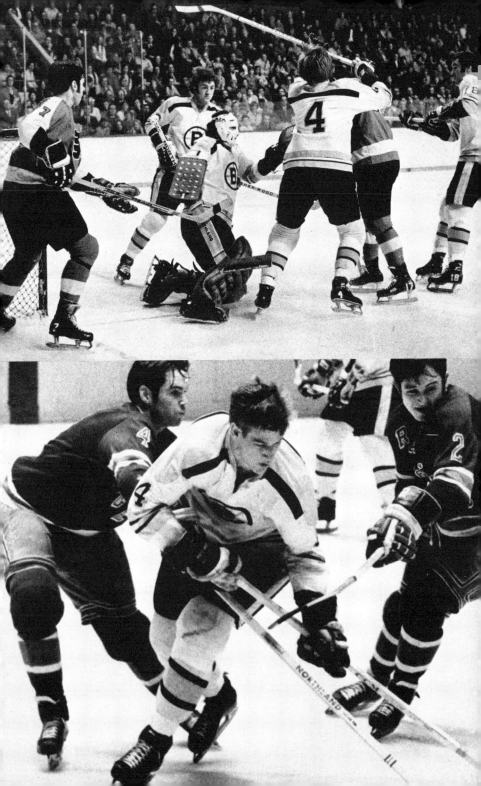

HOCKEY'S
BIGGEST
STAR

Bobby drives in on Montreal
goalie Ken Dryden (above). At
right, he talks to newsmen in
the hospital after his knee
operation in 1972.

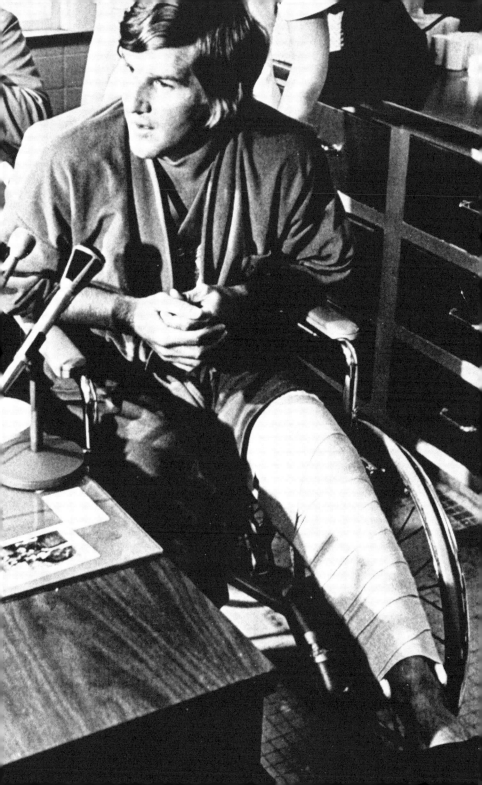

Appointment in Gananoque

There were 70 teenage boys assembled in the large room. A coach wearing a gray sweat shirt and a baseball cap, with a whistle around his neck, stood in front of them. He was the coach of the Oshawa Generals.

The boys, most of them between 16 and 20 years old, had come from all parts of Ontario. Each was the best young hockey player in his town or city. They had been invited to try out for the Generals, one of the toughest amateur hockey teams in Canada. Many would go home disappointed, but a few would show enough promise during this three-day tryout camp to make the team, which was sponsored by the Boston Bruins. Perhaps a few would play so well for Oshawa that they would one day be promoted to the Bruins in the National Hockey League.

Many of the boys looked pale and tense. For some, this was the first time they had been away from home. If they were picked, they would live here in Oshawa, a manufacturing city near Toronto. They would be paid a small allowance —about $10 a week—and would attend a local high school. They would live in the homes of Oshawa families, who would be paid by the Generals for their room and board.

Nearly all the boys were tall and broad-shouldered, their legs thickly muscled from skating since they were three or four. Most of the heavier and taller boys would play defense. You had to be as big as a fullback to bodycheck those fast-flying forwards.

"I'm going to call the roll," the coach announced. "When I call out your name, say 'here.' Then I'll ask you your position."

He began to call out the names. "Robert Orr."

A pipsqueak of a boy—he looked like the waterboy among these fullback-types—shouted, "Here!"

The bigger boys turned to look at the little 14-year-old.

"Position?" asked the coach.

"Defense," squeaked Bobby.

The room shook with laughter.

As long as he could remember, Bobby Orr had heard people—even his own father—say he was too small to be a hockey player. When he was born in Parry Sound on March 20th, 1948, the third child of Doug and Arva Orr, doctors even wondered if he was strong enough to survive. He was soon out of danger, however, and he began to grow—slowly.

Parry Sound is a town of 6,000 people situated at the mouth of the Seguin River on the shores of Georgian Bay. During the winter months, the temperature drops as low as 40 degrees below zero and icy winds whip in from Lake Huron. But in the summer thousands of vacationers from Toronto visit Parry Sound, using its sandy beaches, swimming in the bay, fishing and boating.

Dominating Parry Sound is a huge black railroad trestle that spans the Seguin River and connects the town's two hills. One hill is Belvedere Hill, looking out over Parry Sound. Here the wealthier people live. The other hill is Tower Hill, where the working people live. The Orrs lived in a large, stucco house on Tower Hill.

Doug Orr was a broad-shouldered, crew-cut man who packed explosives at a munitions factory. As a boy of 18, he had been asked to sign a contract with the Boston Bruins. But Canada was at war, and Doug joined the Canadian Navy. He served on a speedy corvette that escorted freighters across the Atlantic, protecting them against attacks from German submarines. When the war was over, Doug felt he was too old for NHL hockey, so he settled down in Parry Sound and began raising a family. Another Parry Sound boy, Pete Horeck, did sign to play pro hockey, and he played ten years with Chicago and Detroit in the NHL. Horeck was about Doug Orr's age, and people in Parry Sound thought Doug was a better player. "Doug was a terrific skater," said one of them. "From a standing start or a face-off, there was no one faster."

Doug Orr continued to play amateur hockey, and his sons, Ron and Bobby, both started skating when they were only three years old. When Bobby first put on skates he looked like a clown in an ice show. "He's skating on his ankles," his father said, laughing. "He takes a stride, falls on his face, gets up and keeps on skating."

A year later, though, little Bobby was swerving across the ice with speed and grace, a tiny hockey stick in his hands. Doug Orr, who played hockey on Saturdays with other men of the town, was watching Bobby one cold, sunny morning. Someone commented on Bobby's ability.

The proud father agreed that Bobby was a good skater. "But I don't think he'll ever make it as a hockey player because he's so bloody small," he said.

Yet at five Bobby was playing for a team in the Minor Squirt League, which is for boys under six. He graduated to the Squirt League when he was six, then through the other age-group leagues: Squirt, Peewee, Bantam, Midget, Juvenile. From there talented boys graduated to Junior Hockey— Junior D, Junior C, Junior B and then Junior A, the jumping-off place to the pros.

Bobby and his friends played league games in the cavernous Parry Sound Memorial Community Center. Sometimes as many as 1,200 half-frozen spectators cheered them on. When they weren't playing organized hockey they played "shinny" on the frozen Seguin River. Often they played with Indian boys, who swung freshly cut saplings for sticks. "Those were hard games," Bobby once said. "You didn't play much unless you could grab the puck and keep it."

One day a group of men watched one of those shinny games. They saw Bobby pick up the puck, skate left, skate right and circle, controlling the puck all the time. No one could knock it away from him.

"What a defenseman he'd make," a man said.

"Too small," said someone else.

When Bobby was ten, his father invited him to play in games against other grown men. Little Bobby sometimes seemed to be racing between the grownups' legs, but even 25-year-old men had trouble cornering the youngster and taking the puck away from him. Parry Sounders stood on the ice and watched Bobby more than they watched the games. Nearly everyone said much the same thing: in a town that had produced excellent hockey players as long as anyone could remember, this was the best young player that Parry Sound had ever seen.

From December through April, with the Seguin frozen, Bobby played shinny, practiced with his teammates, and worked on his fakes (or "dekes"). From early morning until late evening he skated, stick in hand, sometimes skating by himself under the light of the moon.

Not that his life was all hockey. When the snow melted he rode on his bike with his friends down James Street, the main thoroughfare of the town. With his older sisters Pat and Penny, his older brother Ron, and his younger brother Doug,

Bobby attended Sunday School at the Baptist church. He attended the Gibson grammar school. His grades were mostly B's and C's, but he was popular with his teachers, who liked his alert, sparkling personality. In a respectful way, Bobby had a way of making teachers smile and say, "There goes a real good boy."

Often Bobby went for walks in the nearby woods with his grandfather, who talked about playing professional soccer back in Ireland. Bobby wondered what it would have been like if his father had skated for the Bruins or some other NHL team. And he dreamed that one day his father and grandfather might come to Toronto to see him play for an NHL team.

Then he came back down to earth. People were still saying he was too small for Junior Hockey, let alone big league hockey. He would probably be like his dad: playing hockey in Parry Sound on winter weekends, working as a mechanic in Parry Sound or in Toronto, enjoying the good fishing for bass and pickerel out in the blue waters of Georgian Bay during the summer. It was a good, peaceful future to be facing.

In 1959, when Bobby was eleven, he entered the Parry Sound track meet, open to all the school boys in town. Bobby won in the sprints. He won a middle-distance event. He won in several field events. That evening he carried home the trophy awarded to the meet's outstanding athlete.

Bobby set the trophy in a corner of the family living room. Next to it was a trophy awarded to

the track meet's most valuable athlete of 25 years
earlier. The winner of that trophy had been Doug
Orr.

That summer Bobby played shortstop for his
friends' baseball team. He swept up ground balls
like a vacuum cleaner. And he hit towering drives
over the outfielders' heads. He seemed to excel at
any sport he tried.

At eleven Bobby was playing with 14-year-old
boys on the Parry Sound Bantams. Bobby stood
5-foot-2 and weighed only 110 pounds. Yet he was
playing defense. He wasn't knocking forwards
down. When they cruised in toward the net,
Bobby flicked out his stick like a whip and stole
the puck. Then he took off down the ice, the
bigger boys trailing behind him, tongues hanging
out. The Bantams played 60-minute games.
Bobby often played the full 60 minutes, skating up
and down the rink as effortlessly as the wind.

Bucko McDonald was a bull-chested, round-
faced heavyweight, who had played defense in the
NHL for the Detroit Red Wings and the Toronto
Maple Leafs. In 1959 he was the coach of the
Parry Sound hockey program. One day in practice Bucko pointed to young Bobby. "If I've ever
seen an NHL prospect, this kid is one," he said.

"Isn't he too small?" someone replied.

"He'll have to get bigger. But if he does, he
could make it all the way."

Doug Orr once approached McDonald and
suggested that Bobby be switched from defenseman to forward. Bobby was a great scorer,

and besides, Doug had been a forward himself. "The kid is in his natural position," Bucko said emphatically. "Anybody can play forward. He's too smart to be a forward. He belongs on defense." Doug Orr nodded, accepting the coach's decision. But other people wondered: this kid could shoot better than most 18-year-old wingers or centers. Why wasn't he playing center or wing?

Bucko feared that Bobby might be thinking the same way. One day after practice he took Bobby aside and told him, "Look, kid, you'd be better off with defense because forwards are a dime a dozen. Good defensemen are not near as plentiful."

Bobby nodded. But he didn't have to be convinced to play defense. On defense he could play both ends of the ice. It was the perfect position for an all-around player. Someday he would just prove that defensemen could score too.

The Parry Sound Bantams had a great 1959–60 season. In March 1960, just before Bobby turned twelve years old, the Bantams were invited to the All-Ontario Bantam championship tournament, to be held this year in a town called Gananoque, some 200 miles from Parry Sound.

Four worried-looking men were sitting in the offices of the Boston Bruins. Outside, the El trains rumbled past the offices, which were tucked away in Boston Garden, home of the Bruins. It was March 1960, and the Bruin officials—president Weston Adams, general manager Lynn Patrick, and assistants Milt Schmidt and Wren Blair—

were discussing the team. The powerful Bruins had fallen on hard times. They had not even made the 1960 Stanley Cup playoffs. Worse yet, there weren't many promising players coming up for future seasons.

"We need to beat the bushes for new talent," someone said.

Getting new talent was easier said than done in those days. The most promising young players in the Canadian amateur leagues could be "reserved" by a pro team when they were only 14 years old. So unless the Bruin management wanted to make expensive trades, they would have to start looking at prospects who were barely teenagers. Picking a boy that young was risky and it took time—it would be four years or more before a 14-year-old would be ready for play with the Bruins.

Still, the Bruin management decided to take a look at some young talent. The Boston scouts had reported that two promising defensemen would be playing in the Bantam tournament at Gananoque. Their names were Rick Eaton and Doug Higgins. The Bruin officials decided to go to Gananoque and take a look.

The Bruin officials settled into their seats, looking down on the rink as two Bantam teams warmed up by taking practice shots at their goaltender. President Adams and general manager Patrick studied the two defensemen, Eaton and Higgins, who were warming up for the Gananoque Bantams at one end of the ice.

Assistant general manager Milt Schmidt happened to glance at a scrawny kid at the other end of the ice. He had a number two on his back and was warming up for the Parry Sound team. Uniform's too big for him, thought Schmidt. His pants are so big they're hanging below his knees. He doesn't look much more than five feet tall. Must be a confident kid, though, to be out there playing against kids so much bigger.

The game began. Parry Sound swarmed onto the Gananoque ice, led by that little number two. He snapped shot after shot at the cage. He stole the puck. He skated in circles to throw off defenders. Then he winged more shots at the goal.

Scout Wren Blair began to notice number two as well. The Bruin officials didn't even know who the youngster was, but they had already forgotten about Eaton and Higgins. Between periods Blair left his seat and went down to the Parry Sound bench. He talked for a few minutes with one of the grownups from Parry Sound.

When Blair came back, a broad smile covered his face. "That number two is a kid named Orr, Bobby Orr."

Patrick frowned. He wanted to know if any NHL team was sponsoring the Parry Sound Bantams. If so, that NHL team owned the rights to sign Orr.

"Good news," said Blair. "Nobody is sponsoring them."

Patrick and Blair turned back to the game. Parry Sound beat Gananoque. Then in the finals they lost 1–0 to Scarboro. But Bobby Orr played

58 of 60 minutes—so spectacularly that he was the star of the game and the tournament, winning the trophy as the tournament's Most Valuable Player.

Wren Blair was assigned to follow Orr back to Parry Sound. Scouts from the Montreal Canadiens were right behind him. They had also seen that number two in Gananoque. Both teams wanted Bobby to sign a Junior A card—which would mean that the parent team would have exclusive rights to sign him later for play in the NHL. Imagine their surprise when they found out that Bobby was barely twelve years old. He wouldn't be able to sign with a team or play Junior A hockey for two full years! It would be two years of uneasy waiting for all the NHL teams that wanted him.

Wren Blair talked to Parry Sound hockey officials. The Bruins, he said, would donate $1,000 to the town's hockey program. Blair hoped that the $1,000 contribution would make the Orrs think kindly of Boston when the time came for Bobby to sign a Junior card.

Soon the Orr phone was ringing morning, noon and night: Montreal Canadiens calling, Detroit Red Wings calling, Chicago Black Hawks calling. The scouts all wanted to fly to Parry Sound and talk to the Orrs about their son's future as a National Hockey League player—even though little Bobby was only in the seventh grade. His performance at Gananoque had astounded every scout who had seen him.

The most persistent visitor to the Orr home on Tower Hill was Wren Blair. He was coaching the Kingston (Ontario) team, a Boston farm club. He even arranged for the team bus to stop in Parry Sound on road trips. While his players relaxed for an hour or so, Blair talked to the Orrs. He told them that the weak Bruins would give Bobby the quickest route to the NHL.

"I see that Mr. Blair so much," said one neighbor of the Orr family, "I'm beginning to think he's kin."

Bobby's 14th birthday came and went, and he still hadn't signed a Junior A card with an NHL team. But in the summer of 1962 Blair talked Doug and Arva Orr into allowing Bobby to attend a tryout camp for the Oshawa Generals, the Bruins' Junior A team. Most of the players were 16 to 20 years old.

"He'll get knocked around some," Doug told friends. "Then the Bruins and he and I and everyone will know he's not ready yet for that caliber of hockey. Heck, the boy is only in the ninth grade. They want him to go up against players four and five years older."

One Sunday night Bobby clambered aboard a train that sped him 200 miles south to the training camp. When Bobby squeaked that he was a defenseman the bigger boys laughed.

Three days later Doug drove to the camp to bring Bobby home. "We let him go because we thought it would be a holiday for the kid," Doug told a friend on the way down. "But he only weighs 127 pounds. He doesn't have a chance of sticking."

Doug arrived at the camp in time to see a workout. He watched his son speed around the ice and was amazed. "Bobby played a wonderful game," he told people when he and Bobby returned to Parry Sound. "He was stick-handling very well, moving around the others like a weasel."

Bruin officials begged Doug to allow Bobby to sign a Junior A card. Of the some 70 boys at the camp, Bobby had proven to be number one. Wren Blair and his wife drove to Parry Sound and talked to the Orrs. Could Bobby play for Oshawa?

He's too young to leave home, said Mrs. Orr. He's only 14, hardly out of the eighth grade.

But he'll deteriorate as a hockey player if he doesn't play against better opponents, Blair argued.

Oshawa is too far away—150 miles. And he's too small, said Doug Orr, to be checking brawny kids 18, 19 or 20 years old. They'll squash him against the boards with their body checks.

No, he's good enough to play against older boys, said Blair. You saw how he played at the tryout camp. His stickwork and dekes are good enough right now for Bobby to be playing in the NHL.

Bobby was not leaving home, Mrs. Orr said.

He didn't have to leave home, Blair replied

soothingly. The Orrs could drive him to Oshawa for a game, then drive him back home after the game. He wouldn't have to live with strangers in Oshawa, as the other boys were required to do. Sure, it would be a 300-mile round trip. But the trips would be worthwhile. Look what they might do for Bobby's hockey future.

Doug Orr didn't even have a car. He'd have to borrow one. But he turned to Bobby and said, "What do you want to do, Bobby?"

"I'd like to play for Oshawa, dad," Bobby said. He had always known he was a good hockey player, the best in Parry Sound. He had been the best in that tryout camp. Now he would like to see just how good he really was against the best of Canada's amateur hockey players.

Doug Orr turned back to Wren Blair. He agreed to let Bobby play. But if Bobby's health or school grades suffered or if he was overmatched against those older players, he could leave the Generals. Agreed?

Agreed, said Blair. Bobby signed the Junior A card. One day early in the winter of 1962 Bobby stepped into a borrowed car with his father and started out on the road to Oshawa.

YOUNG
BOBBY

The highly publicized young hockey star poses with the Oshawa Generals (left) and with Bruin coach Harry Sinden and fellow rookie Gilles Marotte.

YOUNG BOBBY

Still in his teens, Bobby lines up with the veterans of the Boston Bruins in his first practice.

The Glamour Boy of Canada

Bobby stared wistfully out of the window of the house, looking down on a deserted street in Oshawa. He missed Parry Sound. He wondered what his brother Ron and his sister Pat were doing right now. He often called Pat on the telephone, telling her his problems and asking advice. He thought about his friends in Parry Sound. Ever since they'd been small boys, they had cast for pickerel with a hook at the end of a branch. He thought: I bet the fishing's real good.

Of course, it was nice here in Oshawa. This was his second year with the Generals, and he was 15, going on 16. In his first year, his father had driven him back and forth between Oshawa and Parry Sound. He never even practiced with the team, yet he was named to the league's second all-star team.

At first some of the older players had grumbled about Orr being the coach's pet. The grumbling had ceased when the season began and these rangy 18-year-olds watched the ninth grader display his hockey skills.

"Imagine what he would have done if he'd practiced," the Generals' coach said.

"He amazes me every time I see him," said the Bruins' Lynn Patrick. "The way he can anticipate what's going to happen is sometimes uncanny. He senses where the puck is going to be and moves there even before the puck does."

In this second season with the Generals, the Orrs had allowed Bobby to live in Oshawa. He was enrolled in an Oshawa public high school. He studied technology, specializing in the study of refrigeration.

Bobby was living and eating in the home of Bob and Bernie Elsmere, who had three children. On evenings when there was no game, Bobby came home from practice and played with the children. Sometimes he and other teammates were driven to nearby Toronto to see a movie or a hockey game. It was a fun life.

But this afternoon, staring down from his room at the deserted streets of Oshawa, Bobby felt the twinges of homesickness. He yearned for the cold, clean air of Parry Sound. Suddenly he went to a closet and pulled on a coat and boots. He ran downstairs. He spoke to Bob Elsmere, who smiled and said goodbye. A few minutes later Bobby was driving with a friend toward Parry Sound.

A few hours after Bobby left, a Generals' official phoned the Elsmeres. He wanted to speak to Bobby. To protect Bobby, they said he was asleep. "Good," said the official. "Nothing better for a hockey player than sleep."

That night Bobby was sleeping in the stucco house on Great North Road in Parry Sound. His older sister, Pat, had welcomed him with hugs and tears. His parents asked all the same questions: what was he eating, was he warm enough, did he have enough clothes.

It was good to be back in the midst of this tight-knit family. He missed the closeness that he felt toward Ron, Pat, Penny and young Doug.

"We're a nutty family," Pat once said. "We've all got wild tempers, but we're soft as mush, too. Every time Bobby phones I cry and I can hear him start to blubber, too. I always cry when I see him. Dad thinks we're nuts. We'll all be watching a television program, and I look over to see if Mom's crying and she is. And she looks at me and we both look at Penny and we're all sitting there blubbering. Dad looks at us and just shakes his head."

Bobby grinned, blushing a little when he heard what Patty had said. Sometimes, when he did a dumb thing on the ice—like hitting the puck into a crowd of enemy players—he came off the ice fighting back tears. "Just a blubbering Irishman, that's what I am," he often said.

Now he and his dad were talking about how he was performing for the Generals. He was the youngest player in the league, which was packed with tough players only a jump or two away from the big-time NHL. Bobby was close to a league record for goals by a defenseman. The record was 29, set by Jacques Laperriere, who had gone on to

star with the Montreal Canadiens. Laperriere had
been 20 when he set the record. Bobby was only
15.

Back at Oshawa Bobby reported for practice
after a day at school tinkering with refrigerator
systems. Inside the Generals' clubhouse Bobby
saw pudgy Stan Waylett, the team's trainer. Stan
had become almost a second father to Bobby. The
first day Bobby had walked into the clubhouse he
had felt ill-at-ease—a new boy in a new school.
Stan had greeted him with a bear hug and
welcomed him to the club. Right away Bobby felt
at home.

Now, seeing Stan, Bobby asked for an extra
stick.

"I gave you a stick the other day."

"It broke."

"It broke because you didn't tape it."

"I don't like to tape my sticks. It makes them
heavier."

"Aw! How much can a little tape weigh?"

Bobby grinned. "I guess it's in my head but I
don't like to tape my sticks."

"Then you won't get an extra one from me
until you do."

"Aw, come on Stan."

That night when Bobby arrived at the clubhouse, he found two brand-new sticks in his
locker.

In the next-to-last game of the Generals' season
Bobby batted in three goals—the hat trick—rais-

ing his season's total to 30 goals and breaking Laperriere's record. The news was flashed all across Canada. Canadian hockey fans watch the progress of Junior Hockey stars the way pro football fans in the United States watch All-America football players. An All-America quarterback could be the next Joe Namath; a Junior A hockey star could be the next Bobby Hull.

MacLean's magazine, a national Canadian publication, featured the 16-year-old Bobby on the cover. Dozens of sportswriters visited Oshawa to write about this defenseman who was a unanimous choice on the league's first All-Star team at so young an age.

The Bruins' Wren Blair was concerned. He told an American visitor: "Hockey players are Canada's glamor boys. They get a kind of Hollywood adulation. . . . In the smaller papers they get more space than the prime minister, particularly young Orr, who, because of his extreme youth, has been getting incredible publicity for three years now. I mean, playing Junior A hockey at fourteen—that alone is enough to attract wide attention. So I've drummed it into him over and over that it's his responsibility to be level-headed enough to handle it.

"You'd be surprised at how many hero-worshipers there are. Even businessmen in big cities pander to name athletes just to be seen in their company. They wine and dine a good athlete, wanting to be seen by their friends with a celebrity. Sure, it's a free ride for the athlete, but he'll wind up a bum if he doesn't learn to handle those fair-weather friends."

Someone asked Bobby about all the publicity he was receiving. "I try not to read about myself," he said. "So many people have told me not to get a swelled head that I'm scared to read the stuff . . ."

Bobby was now boarding with Cora and Jack Wild. The Wilds agreed: all the publicity had not inflated Bobby's ego. "You've never seen a boy so polite," said Mrs. Wild. "I remember telling a friend about him once, and she insisted no boy could be as perfect as I described. Then she met Bob—and agreed. . . ."

Bobby returned in the spring to Parry Sound. He played shortstop for a local baseball team. He also played lacrosse so well that a pro team in Oshawa offered him a tryout.

"A good hockey player can play all games well," said Wren Blair, adding that Gordie Howe often worked out with the Detroit Tigers. A fight promoter once saw Howe stripped to his waist and commented that with such a build Howe could be a heavyweight champion.

"The point is," Wren Blair continued, "every hockey player must have the attributes of the top athletes in any game." He must have speed, agility, strength and quick reflexes, Wren said, "and then he must add the encumbrance of skates." If you can play good hockey, Blair seemed to say, you are going to be good at any game played on solid footing.

To add to the family income, Bobby worked summers in Parry Sound and winters in Oshawa. One summer he was a $35-a-week clerk in Adam's Men's Wear shop on Parry Sound's main street. "He lost money on that deal," said his sister Pat. He spent so much on clothes that he had nothing left.

Bobby also worked in his uncle's butcher shop on James Street. The pay was $25 a week and all the meat he could take home. One day, slicing bacon, he almost cut off his thumb. That night, his hand bandaged, he met his mother outside the butcher shop. "Looking at you," she said tartly, "I think you cut more fingers than meat."

Girls from all over called him in Oshawa and Parry Sound, asking for dates. They lined up outside his house, asking for autographs. Bobby dated only a few girls. "The type of girl who calls you," he said to a friend, "isn't the kind I would want to take out anyway."

Bobby was sitting in Joe Bolahood's sporting goods store in Oshawa, talking with some of his teammates a few days before the start of the 1965–66 season. Most of the Generals thought they had a good enough team to battle for the Memorial Cup, the Stanley Cup of Junior A hockey. While the boys were talking, Joe Bolahood came over and asked Bobby to go out and fetch him a hamburger and coffee.

"Sure," Bobby said, getting up and taking the coins that Joe handed him.

There was an impish grin on Bobby's long face
as he hurried across the street to a restaurant. He
bought the hamburger and coffee. But on the way
back he took out the hamburger and put a
rolled-up paper napkin in its place.

"Here you are, Joe," he said, handing Bolahood
his "hamburger," coffee and change.

"Thanks, Bobby," Joe said, busy with a cus-
tomer.

A few minutes later, still talking to the cus-
tomer, Joe unwrapped the hamburger and bit
into it. As he chewed, a puzzled look crossed his
face. He looked down at the hamburger, saw the
rolled-up paper, and began to spit out what he
had been chewing.

Outside the store window Bobby was watching
through the glass and laughing and laughing and
laughing.

Little Bobby Orr wasn't so little any more.
Each year he was creeping up on boys his age. At
17 he stood 5-foot-10 and packed 175 pounds of
muscle. He had been lifting barbells for 45
minutes every morning. He pressed handgrips to
strengthen his wrists and arms. In the afternoons
during the summer he ran four miles around the
shore of Parry Sound.

He was still the acrobatic skater and stick-handler who dazzled both opponents and teammates.
The Rangers' general manager, Emile Francis,
came to Oshawa to see him play. Later Francis
told someone: "His teammates would give him
the puck, then they'd stand around and watch

him in amazement."

By now Bobby's fame had spread to NHL cities in the United States. In Boston glum Bruin fans were lustily booing a last-place team. Bruin officials tried to perk up their hopes by boasting of Bobby. "We can't sign him to a pro contract until he is eighteen," new general manager Hap Emms told newspapermen. "He's only a Junior A hockey player right now but I wouldn't trade him for the entire Toronto Maple Leaf team."

That sounded like an exaggeration to some people in Boston. But in Oshawa there were people who said: "I wouldn't trade Bobby Orr for the entire Toronto Maple Leaf team *and* the entire Boston Bruin team."

In the 1964–65 season the 16-year-old Bobby had whipped home 34 goals and collected 59 assists for 93 points—the highest total of any defenseman in the history of the Ontario Hockey Association. In the 1965–66 season he scored 37 goals and 60 assists, breaking his own record.

"He not only seems to know what the opposing defense is going to do when he's on the attack," said his coach, Bep Guidolin, "but his judgment on defense is positively uncanny. It's almost like he had a magnet on the end of his stick, the way he attracts that puck."

"He could go into the NHL right now," Hap Emms said of 17-year-old Bobby. "But we have to wait until his 18th birthday—March 20th, 1966."

By early March of 1966 the Generals had won the Ontario Hockey Association Junior A championship. They skated onto the ice for the Memorial Cup finals, a best-of-seven series against the Edmonton Oil Kings for the Junior championship of Canada.

Ads for the championship games skipped over the teams. Instead they focused on Bobby:

"SEE BOSTON'S $1,000,000 PROSPECT, BOBBY ORR."

"YOUR LAST CHANCE TO SEE BOBBY ORR PLAY JUNIOR HOCKEY."

In their Boston office, the Bruin officials talked about Bobby and the Memorial Cup.

"Tell Bep Guidolin he shouldn't play Orr," one man said. "He's got a bad knee. Suppose he really hurts it? It could kill the Bruins. Fans are expecting him to lead this team back to respectability."

Of course, the Bruins had yet to sign Bobby. Although they had the rights to him, they still had to agree on a contract with him. But young hockey players weren't used to big money. The Bruins didn't seem worried—Bobby would sign for a small bonus and a minimum salary, they felt.

Bruin general manager Hap Emms flew to Toronto for the Memorial Cup games. Orr was limping noticeably off the ice, and he skated at only three-quarter speed during the first five games. Edmonton led Oshawa three games to two and needed only one more victory for the championship.

In Bobby's hotel room before the sixth game,

Emms said, "Don't play, Bobby. You could end your career."

"No. I owe it to all the guys to play. I want to win the championship."

In his stern, schoolmasterish way, Emms told Bobby he would not play. Orr said he would. Bobby went with the team to Maple Leaf Gardens.

Outside the dressing room Emms met Doug Orr.

"I don't want that boy to play," Emms snapped.

"Bobby wants to play. And that's good enough for me."

"He's not going to play," roared Emms.

"Now, wait a minute Mr. Emms," Doug said in a cold, measured voice. "Bobby still doesn't belong to the Bruins. He's my son. Just remember that."

Emms walked away.

That night Bobby clambered off the boards to try to play on the sore knee. The first time he skated onto the ice, he fell down. He got up and skated, the pain showing on his face. "You never saw so many women crying in the stands," said Cora Wild, Bobby's "mother" in Oshawa. "We all knew how much pain Bob was in."

Bep Guidolin waved Bobby off the ice. But when Bep turned his back, Bobby leaped back into the game. "He can't hardly walk," a team-mate said, "and look at him trying to skate."

Someone knocked Bobby down. He tried to get

up, and fell. Then he got up slowly, wincing, and went on skating. With Bobby half-crippled, the Generals lost the game and the championship series.

After the game the crowd stood and applauded the winning Edmonton team—and then Bobby. "I never saw a kid display more guts than Bobby did tonight," Doug Orr said to a friend.

Newspaper reporters flooded into Hap Emms' office in Boston one spring day in 1966. "The Orr family has hired a lawyer to negotiate his contract," one reporter said to Emms. "What will you do?"

"I won't deal with a lawyer," Emms said. "We have offered him a sum that is absolutely our best—a $5,000 bonus and an $8,000 salary. After all, the boy has to prove himself. He hasn't played big league hockey. He scored a lot of goals rushing up the ice from defense in Junior Hockey. A lot of people say he'll never be allowed to do that in the NHL. We've got big men up here who may knock him down when he rushes."

In Parry Sound the Orrs conferred with their lawyer, Alan Eagleson, a canny negotiator. Eagleson told reporters that Bobby might play with the amateur National Hockey Team of Canada if he didn't get a suitable offer from the Bruins.

By mid-August Emms was sweltering—and not from the summer heat. Everywhere he heard the talk of excited Bruin fans: "We want Orr—the heck with the cost."

The fans had sat too long through losing seasons. "If the Bruins don't sign Orr," one newspaperman cracked, "the fans won't do anything except burn down Boston Garden."

It was early September. Hap Emms was cruising on Lake Huron in his 42-foot cabin cruiser. Standing at the wheel, peering through the spray, he saw the tall fir trees rising like slender sentries on the sandy shore. He slowed the engine, cruised to a marina dock, and cut off the engine.

He looked at his watch. In a few minutes the Orrs and their lawyer, Alan Eagleson, would arrive from nearby Parry Sound. Hap Emms had agreed to sit down with the Orrs' lawyer. The Bruins would be reporting to training camp in a few weeks. And the uproar in Boston was growing louder: He had to sign Orr.

Bobby, his father, some friends and Eagleson walked down the dock and came on board. Then night settled over the lurching cruiser and the men talked under swinging lanterns. They talked until well past midnight.

Eagleson was asking more than $30,000 a year for Orr, an unproven junior. Emms argued that only Bobby Hull, Gordie Howe and Jean Beliveau were earning $40,000 a year. Eagleson answered by ticking off the $100,000 bonuses being paid for football, baseball and basketball rookies. Why couldn't pro hockey match the bonuses being paid by other pro sports?

Just before two o'clock in the morning Emms

walked down the gangplank to the dock and placed a call to the Bruins' owner in Boston. A little later he came back and he and Bobby Orr shook hands. For some $30,000 a year, Bobby Orr would sign a two-year contract with the Boston Bruins.

That September night Bobby rode home to Parry Sound in triumph. "I think I did something that will be good for all the players someday," he said later. "I just stood up, eh? I don't think they can mind that."

The next day Bobby Hull heard about Orr's $30,000-a-year contract. "Orr and Al Eagleson have done a wonderful thing for every player in hockey," Hull said. "Now we are going to be paid the kind of money that football and baseball have been paying. Because if Orr is getting $30,000, the owners have to pay me and Howe a lot more than $40,000. They have got to pay every hockey player a lot more money."

During the next few weeks hockey buffs talked about little except Bobby Orr. Was he *really* all that good? Sure, he had been a ball of fire in Junior Hockey. But now he would come to the big time watched by every NHL veteran. He'd be checked, slammed, knocked down, bruised, elbowed, kneed. Would he be able to race around unmolested as he had done in Junior Hockey?

"I know I can't do all the things I've done," Bobby told a friend one day. "I guess there'll be a lot of sleepless nights for me if I don't live up."

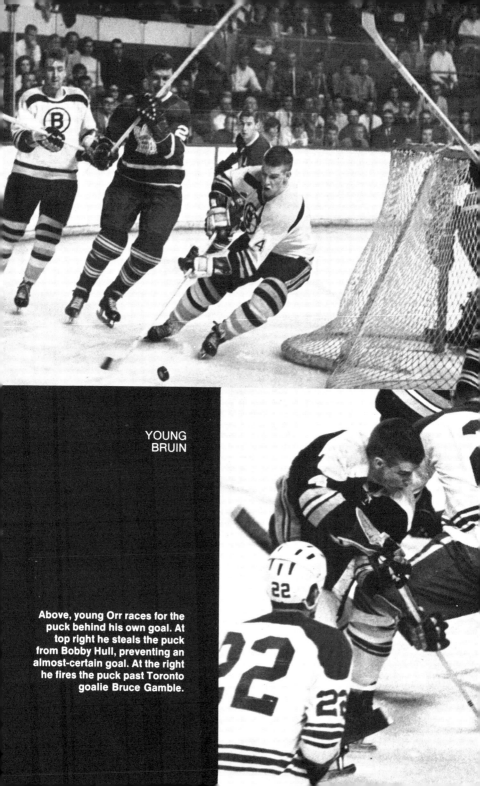

YOUNG BRUIN

Above, young Orr races for the puck behind his own goal. At top right he steals the puck from Bobby Hull, preventing an almost-certain goal. At the right he fires the puck past Toronto goalie Bruce Gamble.

"Eighteen Speeds of Fast"

Bobby caught the puck on his stick, veered to his left, and skated up ice toward his own blue line. He saw a Ranger cutting in front of him.

"Bob, Bob," hissed a voice behind him. "I've got a clear shot. Drop the puck."

Bobby dropped the puck behind him. Then, hearing the crowd's sudden roar, he turned around. The player who had hissed at him was wearing a blue shirt. He was a Ranger—Vic Hadfield. Hadfield streaked toward the startled Bruin goalie, shot—and scored.

Red-faced, Orr skated to his bench. He had been tricked by Hadfield and made a dumb rookie's mistake. He sat down on the bench, and buried his face in his hands.

Bobby didn't make too many dumb rookie mistakes in this 1966–67 season. He was playing before Bruin fans and players who had been told for years that he was a Hall-of-Fame player.

Bruin fans half-expected him to lift the Bruins to first place on his sinewy shoulders.

No one could lift this team to first place all by himself. But Bobby Orr did not disappoint anyone with his play. In his very first game, against the Detroit Red Wings at Boston Garden, he broke up attack after attack by poking the puck away from a forward or dropping to his knees to sweep away a shot. The Bruins won 6–2, and Bobby had one assist. Fans poured down a tumultuous welcome as he came off the ice.

A few days later he skated up ice against the Montreal Canadiens, crossed the blue line, swept back his stick and slapped the puck.

It whizzed off the ice and rocketed toward the cage. The Canadien goalie dove, skates first, toward the corner of the cage. But he was too late, and the puck flew into the corner of the nets. Bobby Orr had scored his first NHL goal.

The crowd in Boston Garden stood and applauded for several minutes. The 18-year-old skated below them in small circles, head down, embarrassed. Montreal coach Toe Blake said later, "I never heard anything like it."

Wren Blair sat in the Bruin dressing room, talking to Bobby before a game. "There's gonna be players who resent you," Blair said as Bobby listened, tight-lipped. "Don't back off. If they want to fight, throw off your gloves and go at them. Let them know right away where you stand. There are few players who really want to fight. If you show them you want to fight, they'll get the message in a hurry. Get it over with so that you're not hampered by that nonsense too long. Then let your hockey ability take over."

A few weeks later Bobby bumped into Canadien defenseman Ted Harris, one of the league's toughest fist fighters. Harris said something. Orr shouted something right back. Both threw off their gloves. Harris charged, and Bobby flicked out a right. Down went Harris.

He jumped up, surprised by the quickness of that right, and ploughed into Bobby once more. Out snapped another right and down went Harris again.

Officials stopped the fight and Bobby went back to playing hockey.

After the game he grinned and said, "It's amazing what you can do when you're scared."

He paused. "I'd rather play hockey," he said, "but I'll never back away. If you do they'll run you right out of the league."

Bobby was now 6 feet tall and weighed 185 pounds. He was still willowy but he was deceptively strong, as opponents soon learned. In one game Gordie Howe, the possible heavyweight champ, collided with Bobby in a corner. Bobby picked Howe off the ice and flung him down as though he were a sack of potatoes. No one talked any more about Bobby being too small—it was clear he was big enough to do the job.

He had come to the Bruins calling the other players "sir" and "mister." At first he was shocked at how they ribbed each other. Sometimes, when one player was yelling insults at the other, he thought fists would be flying. Instead each broke up into laughter.

He got his share of kidding about all the money he was earning. Once he came out of his hotel room carrying a large package. A teammate, Ron Stewart, saw him.

"Hey, Bobby," Stewart yelled, some other players turning to watch. "What's that you're carrying—your money for the week?"

Everyone laughed. Bobby flushed. But he soon learned how to needle back, knowing that this was all in good fun and a way of cementing friendships.

His one big test came shortly after he joined the team. The veterans of NHL teams often "haze" a new player, and the Bruins were no exception. They caught Bobby, dragged him to the locker room, stripped him and shaved him from head to foot with a dull razor. It was painful and humiliating for Bobby, but he made no complaint. This was his initiation into the brutal side of hockey, and he passed the test.

He quickly impressed the Bruins with his skills. In one practice session, he zigzagged backward as a Bruin forward brought up the puck. Suddenly Bobby stopped, lashed out with his stick and stole the puck.

Now he was racing up the ice, zipping across the center line. A defenseman, Ted Green, came up to meet him. Bobby deked to the left, flashed his stick to the right, seemed to rise up on the front of his blades and tap-dance around the bewildered Green. He came down again and reached out his long arms to put the puck back on his stick. He wiggled the puck on the stick, faking the goalie toward the left corner of the net, then swatted the puck for a bull's-eye hit into the top right corner.

After the play Green skated over to Bobby. "Kid," said the veteran defenseman, "whatever they're paying you, it isn't enough."

Veteran hockey watchers were coming to Boston Garden to stare entranced at this phenom. A former U.S. Olympic star, Bill Cleary, was sitting in Boston Garden one evening with newspaperman Chris Lydon. "Watch him now," Cleary said as Bobby circled behind his own net in pursuit of the puck. "Most defensemen would be skating hellbent for the puck, but he's looking to both sides and behind him as he goes, checking out the whole team. He'll have an offensive play in his head before he reaches the puck."

The key word about Orr, Lydon noted, is "anticipation." Later he wrote: "He sees all the action on the ice and knows where everyone is going to be moments before they get there. He thinks of passes that occur to nobody else. Like Bob Cousy in his early days with the [basketball] Celtics, he hits open men who didn't realize they were open and weren't ready to receive a pass."

Ranger coach Emile Francis grinned wryly after Bobby had helped to beat the Rangers with two goals and two assists. "I saw a lot of him as a junior," Francis said. "The kids would give him the puck and then they'd stand around and watch him. In the pros I figured they'd throw the puck to him and then set themselves up for a return pass. That's what happened.

"I've looked at my scoring sheet after each Boston game and there's Orr with six, seven, eight shots. In one game he's got 12 shots. Heck, he's a defenseman. He's not supposed to get that many shots. I figure that since he's a defenseman, maybe he should spend more time defending. But I try to think how many times we've caught him for a goal and I can't find it happening too often. . . ."

Everyone—his coach, his teammates, opponents, writers, fans—were busy that season of 1966–67 dissecting the style of this 18-year-old. Experts raved about his skating. "You may have noticed," said Bruin coach Harry Sinden, "that Bobby skates with his feet fairly far apart. Most sound skaters are a little bowlegged, which is good because it gives them better balance."

"Bobby is deceptive," said Bruin official Milt Schmidt. "He has two speeds. And it doesn't take him the usual three, four or five strides to accelerate from one speed to another. One stride, and he's away."

Ted Green disagreed with his boss. "He's got 18 speeds of fast," Green said, "and I don't think he's yet reached his fastest speed."

The classic defenseman had been a slow, fullback type who knocked down forwards with checks or pinned them to the boards. Although he was strong, Bobby didn't often use brute strength to stop a rushing forward. "To check a guy, you don't have to run him through the boards," he told a friend. "Sometimes I hit, but not that often. I just take the man out by getting in front of him so he can't get by me, or so that the only way he can get by is by going over the top, and that is pretty tough."

"It's no disadvantage for Orr not to be a rough checker," said Gordie Howe after a game with the Bruins. "He can still take you out of a play better than any guy on that team."

"Defensively," said the Rangers' Jean Ratelle, "he's got all the moves. I always have to be careful with him because he can block my shot and get the puck away from me in the same move."

Bobby sometimes seemed to be blocking as many shots as a goalie, dropping fearlessly to the ice to catch that half-pound hunk of rubber on his chest, his legs, arms or stick—always hoping that hunk of rubber wouldn't rip into his face.

"If Bobby has a problem," Boston goaltender Gerry Cheevers once said, "it's just that he has no fear. No fear whatever. If nothing else will do, I swear he'll use his head to block a shot. He won't play it safe."

When he did get hit, the injury didn't stop him. In one game against Montreal a puck punched a hole an inch above Bobby's right eye. The next morning the eye was a purplish ball and shut tight. That night Bobby skated onto the ice to play the Canadiens again. Before the game Bobby told writer Stan Fischler: "I feel bad. I wish there was no game. But it's a funny thing. Sometimes you play your best on days like this."

Bobby was skating one-eyed against the Stanley Cup champions. Early in the game a Canadien forward skated toward the net and walloped the puck at the corner. But Bobby wasn't puck-shy. He dived, and the puck hit his leg and bounced away.

Later in the game, the score tied, 4–4, one-eyed Bobby picked up the puck and sped across the blue line into Montreal territory. Two forwards cut across to intercept him, but Bobby twisted by.

"He gives them that one-two circle dance of his, that ballerina twirl," a Bruin once said, "and he's moving in on the net at top speed."

Montreal's Ted Harris rushed up to check Bobby. Orr deked and Harris checked empty air. Bobby closed in on the Montreal net from the right side. The Montreal goaltender lunged to the right. Bobby sped right by, circled the net, and flew around to the left side.

With that one seeing eye he saw a crack, no more than five inches wide, between the goal-tender's skate and the goalpost. Bobby shoved the puck through the crack and into the nets for a goal.

Bobby thrust his stick high into the air, the traditional gesture of the goal-scorer. The Bruins rushed up to him, slapping him on the rump with their sticks.

"That kid ain't human," one said to another.

Hockey men poured down praise on this astonishing rookie. "What can Orr do?" said Milt Schmidt. "The question is: What can't Orr do?"

"Hockey is a game of mistakes," said Teddy Green. "And Bobby doesn't make any. It's as simple as that."

Yet one distinguished name—Bobby Hull—thought he saw a chink in the Orr armor. "Last year," Hull wrote at the end of Bobby's rookie season, "Bobby was often caught out of position defensively because he rushed so deep into the other end that he couldn't get back to his own zone in time. When one defenseman is out of position, it places a heavier burden on his partner. That's why Gilles Marotte, who played beside Orr last winter, was beaten for so many goals—he was left alone too often to handle two- and three-man rushes."

Veteran Boston goaltender Eddie Johnston disagreed with Hull. He didn't think those end-to-end rushes by Orr hurt the Bruin defense. Instead, they helped, he said. "What people forget," he told a reporter, "is that when Orr has the puck, the other team can't score no matter how far he rushes with it. You can't score if you don't have the puck. He controls the puck for maybe ten, fifteen, twenty minutes a game. He slows down the game, he speeds it up. And if you can keep the puck away from the other side, you are depriving them of ten, fifteen or twenty minutes when they can't shoot and score."

Some veteran defensemen saw minor errors in Bobby's defensive playing. "Sometimes," said the

Rangers' Harry Howell, "I've seen him look down at the puck instead of keeping his eyes on a guy's chest when he's coming at you. I'd say that right now he's got 75 percent of his defense worked out. The rest will come in two or three years."

Bobby himself was conscious of some of his failings. In one game he streaked the length of the rink to whack in a goal. But on the face-off Bobby Hull and Dennis Hull teamed to deke him out of position and slam home a tying goal.

Mortified at being fooled, Bobby skated to the bench and slumped down with his head hanging on his chest. He stared at his skates. He didn't want people to see his face. He was crying with rage.

Near the end of the season Bobby ranked third among the Bruin scorers. Some fans wondered: why not start Bobby at center? It was the old argument: he was a great passer and playmaker and he would score even more goals.

Coach Sinden disagreed. The Bruins, he said, would give up more goals if Bobby played at forward. "Sure," Sinden said, "Bobby might score two goals a game instead of one a game if he played forward. But if we give up four goals a game instead of two, what have we gained? Nothing. We've lost. There's no sense taking the game's best defenseman and playing him in another position," Sinden added. "It makes as much sense as playing Elizabeth Taylor in a boy's role."

Bobby didn't want to play any other position

except defense. "What I enjoy most about playing defense," he told a friend, "is that you're facing the play all the time. You can't do that in any other position. If a forward loses the puck, he has to turn and lose sight of what's happening."

Bobby knew that sometimes he even played too much defense trying to be both defenseman and goaltender. "I back in too far on our goalkeeper," he told a reporter one afternoon after practice, sipping a cup of coffee. "I keep trying to remind myself to stay up at the blue line, forcing the guy to commit himself sooner. I don't mind blocking shots, but if I back in too far I'm apt to screen our goalkeeper. And, anyway, it's better if I can force the other guy to make his move when he's well out."

Bobby was learning what he could do and what he should not do. There was, for example, the problems of checking the bull-like Golden Jet— Bobby Hull.

"To guard Bobby Hull, I've learned you got to spring some surprise moves on him," he said near season's end. "But mostly it's tight checking. You've got to stay close to him and check him hard. I have to make him realize that he's got to shoot from the blue line—or else. That 'else' is me. Hull's shot rises so fast that if you're ten feet away and try to block it with your knees, it'll rise up and take your head off. You can't be bashful about checking Hull."

Bobby checked the 210-pound Golden Jet so hard that Hull often came off the ice shaking his head. "Running into Orr," Hull said one day, "is like getting hit by a pickup truck."

Bobby won the Calder Memorial Trophy as the league's rookie of the year. "I think he's the best rookie I've ever seen," said Chicago coach Billy Reay, who had seen Hull and Howe and Beliveau as rookies. Bobby scored 13 goals and assisted on 28 others for 41 points, third highest among the Bruins.

The winner of the James Norris Trophy, as the league's best defenseman, was the Ranger veteran, Harry Howell. Receiving the silver trophy, Howell hugged it to his chest and told the audience at the awards ceremony, "I might as well enjoy it now because I expect it's going to belong to Bobby Orr for the next ten years."

The coming of Orr, however, had not lifted the Bruins out of the basement. For the sixth time in seven years, they finished last. The fans didn't blame Bobby, they blamed the rest of the Bruins.

In one game Bobby was skating rings around opponents. "Hey, Sinden," a Bruin fan yelled at the coach. "Get that Orr outta the game. He's making the rest of your players look bad."

BOSTON ON THE RISE

Boston's big guns for th
1968–69 season: Derek (Turk
Sanderson, high-scoring Ph
Esposito, and third-yea
defenseman Bobby Or

Bruin goalie Ed Johnston is down on the ice as Bobby races Chicago's Pit Martin for the puck in a 1967 game. At the right Bobby helps Johnston fasten his mask in place.

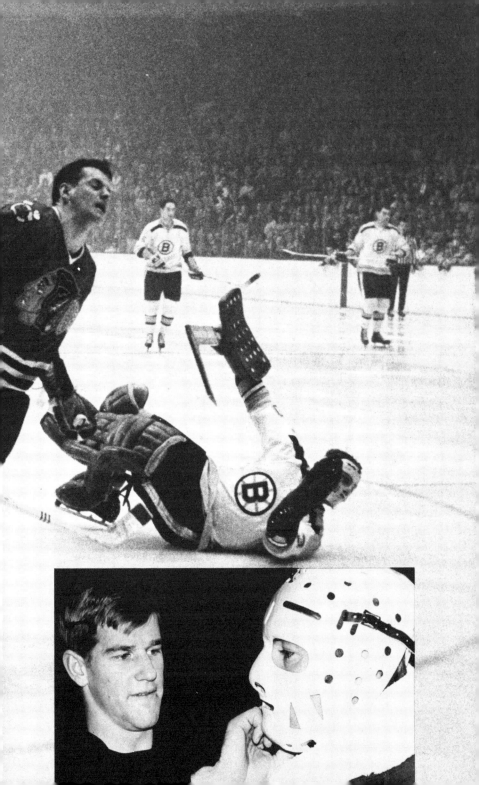

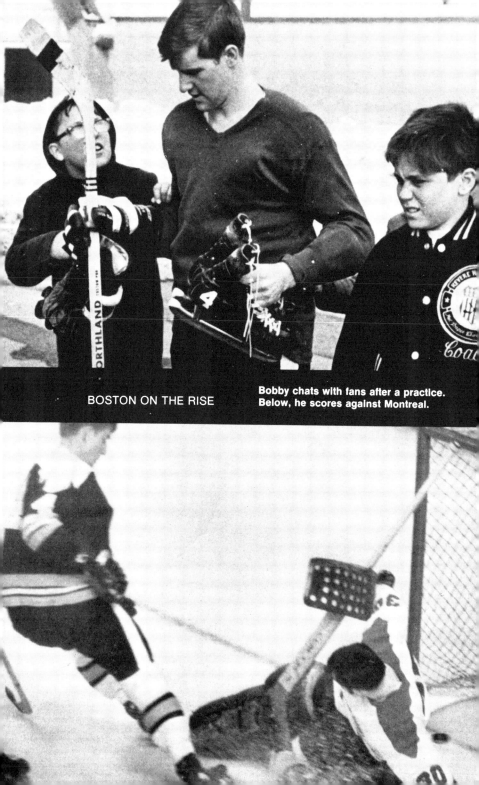

BOSTON ON THE RISE

Bobby chats with fans after a practice.
Below, he scores against Montreal.

Washed Up
at Twenty?

The puck flew toward Bruin goaltender Gerry Cheevers. He flicked out his glove, caught it and dropped it onto the ice. He saw number four, Bobby Orr, bursting away from a gang of players at the blue line.

Cheevers batted the puck to Orr, who caught it cleanly on his stick. Bobby darted across the Detroit blue line. He was yards ahead of two Detroit pursuers. Bobby turned his head to look back, as though looking for another Bruin.

Goaltender Roger Crozier swiveled his head, looking for that other Bruin. As Crozier let down his guard, Bobby—still looking backward—slapped a rising shot that bulleted over Crozier's shoulder and into the net.

In this 1967–68 season, Bobby's second in the NHL, the Bruins wore a new look. No longer did they look like rag-tag losers. They had a look of winners.

First there was Orr, scoring goals and blocking shots. At training camp goaltender Eddie Johnston dusted off an old joke. "He blocks so many shots I should give him half my salary," Johnston said. "Except that with all the money he makes, he doesn't need it."

Then there were new faces. One was the swarthy, often-angry face of Phil Esposito. A tall dock-walloper of a center, Phil had skated for the Chicago Black Hawks—a winning team. "You've become accustomed to losing," he raged at the Bruins during team meetings. "You can win, but you got to *want* to win."

Coming with Esposito in the trade with the Black Hawks were the brawny Ken Hodge and tough Fred Stanfield who would provide the muscle Boston needed to penetrate enemy defenses. A few seasons later Hodge would team up with Esposito and Wayne Cashman to form the highest-scoring line in NHL history.

Another new face was 21-year-old Derek Sanderson, who strutted into camp and told most everyone he would be the rookie of the year. If you laughed, Derek might sit you down with a lightning right to the jaw. Derek liked to fight, but he was also a speedy skater with a stick as quick as an adder's tongue. On face-offs, when the referee dropped the puck, Derek nearly always tapped the puck to a teammate. Winning face-offs is one sign of a good center. Right from the start Derek was winning three of every four.

The leader of the team in earlier years was Terrible Teddy Green, who would actually punish a teammate with his fists if he didn't think he was trying hard enough. Now Phil Esposito provided additional leadership.

A third natural leader was Bobby Orr. He was so much younger that he could hardly take charge, yet Bobby knew that the players looked to him on the ice—to get the puck, to pass the puck, to shoot the puck. Off the ice Bobby had some responsibility to lead, too.

Early in the 1967–68 season two Bruins were feuding. "If this keeps up," Bobby told a teammate, "the team will be split—some guys siding with one guy, the others taking the side of the other guy. In no time we'll have a team divided by dissension."

One morning, just before practice, Bobby walked to the center of the clubhouse and called out the names of the two feuding players.

"You have your choice of weapons for a duel," Bobby said, grinning. He held in his hand a paper bag. He pulled out a water pistol, a pair of baby-sized boxing gloves and finally a toy cannon.

The team roared with laughter. The two feuding players grinned, glanced at each other—and the feud was over.

The new season had gotten off to a bad start for Bobby. In a preseason All-Star game he tore ligaments in his right knee.

"You weren't supposed to play in that game," a Bruin official roared at Bobby when he came to training camp.

"I was wrong," Bobby said. "But after all, it

was a charity game for old-time players."

Then in December, skating against the Maple Leafs, Bobby was dropped by a body check thrown by burly Frank Mahovlich. He got up with a broken collarbone and a separated shoulder.

He returned to action a few weeks later, still aching but insisting he could play. Coach Harry Sinden watched him skate during a practice one morning.

"I've never seen him when he isn't trying to live up to his reputation," Sinden said to a newspaperman. "What this means is: he won't tell anyone when he's injured. Unless you catch him off-guard, or some bones are broken, you never know if he's hurt. All he ever says is, 'I'm all right, I'm all right.' "

In January Bobby was playing in his first NHL All-Star game. He burst across the midline with the puck. Pete Stemkowski slammed into him and Bobby dropped to the ice.

Watching were Milt Schmidt and Harry Sinden. "He's hurt his shoulder!" Sinden yelled.

"Take him out of the game! Take him out of the game!" Schmidt yelled at All-Star coach Toe Blake. "He's hurt! He's hurt!"

Blake did not pull Bobby out of the game. He couldn't believe Bobby was hurt—not the way he was blocking shots and shooting the puck. With less than a minute to play Bobby snapped a shot that narrowly missed tying the game.

That night Bobby could not lift his arm. His

shoulder was injured and he missed five games.

A month later he hurt his other knee—the left knee. Bruin fans were beginning to call him Brittle Bob. "The name and the injuries are something I'll have to get used to," he said, showing no annoyance. "People tell me I'm brittle, but I can't afford to think things like this. I won't let it affect my play. I only wish there was a 'brittle test' so I can know once and for all what the story is—am I brittle or not?"

A few days later he stepped onto the ice in Detroit's Olympia Stadium. As he cruised across the ice the left knee locked as straight as a board. Bobby hobbled off the ice. This was one injury he couldn't hide. He couldn't play. Not any more.

He was flying in a jet some 30,000 feet high, staring down at clouds that looked like puffy pillows. He didn't want to think about what awaited him when the plane landed in Boston: a visit to a hospital and then surgery on the left knee.

He was worried. He had been lucky as far as injuries went. Sure, he'd broken his nose a half-dozen times, but he had seldom been cut, needing only about 25 stitches in his career. Some guys needed that many after one or two games. And unlike many players, he still owned all his teeth.

But now maybe he was through. Maybe Bobby Orr, only 20 years old, was washed up, finished.

The plane droned toward Boston and an operating room.

Some six weeks later, after surgeons had called the operation "completely successful," Bobby tried to play. The Bruins needed him. They were fighting desperately to get into the playoffs for the first time in eight years.

Before his first game Bobby swallowed nervously. "I just don't know how I'm going to feel after this one," he told a friend. "It's like a guy going into his first game ever."

Harry Sinden didn't want to put Bobby on the ice too often. He knew he would be rusty after a six-week layoff. The game began. The Red Wings swarmed in on the Boston cage like so many hornets.

"You wonder what you can do to swing the pendulum," Sinden said later. "You look along the bench and there he is and you say, 'Bob, get out there!' And suddenly you've changed the whole flow."

The Bruins won the game and finished third in 1967–68—a giant leap upward for a team that had languished so long in the league basement. They qualified for the playoffs, but were eliminated in the first round by Montreal in four straight games.

Yet there was a new cockiness about the team. "In two years," Phil Esposito was telling people, "this team is going to win the Stanley Cup."

Injuries had slowed down Bobby and kept him off the ice for almost a third of the season. He had scored only 11 goals and assisted on 20 others for a total of 31 points—10 fewer than his rookie season. But when he had played, even hobbled by pain, he skated with a brilliance that made people's eyes pop. He won—for the first time—the James Norris Trophy as the league's outstanding defenseman.

Strange sounds were clicking in Bobby's knee. In May he went to see the doctor. X-rays showed a cartilage chip in the knee. In June the doctor cut into the knee a second time and removed the chip. All that summer Bobby hobbled around Parry Sound on crutches. At night, alone, he wondered: could he come back? was he through?

Every few days he drove to Toronto and sat in a whirlpool bath. He hoped the baths would help to make the knee strong again. One afternoon in September, only a few weeks to go before the start of the 1968–69 season, he was in the whirlpool talking to writer Stan Fischler about how his fame had made him a marked man in Parry Sound.

"I'm almost afraid to go back to Parry Sound after the season," he said. "You know how it is—you're walking along the street and don't notice someone. The next thing you know word gets around: 'Orr has gone snooty on us. He doesn't even say hello to his home-town people any more' . . ."

That afternoon Bobby and Fischler would drive back to Parry Sound. Bobby was wearing a red-and-blue striped tie, a mod blue-striped suit and wrap-around sunglasses. He reminded Fischler of movie star Warren Beatty.

Bobby walked briskly to his car after the whirlpool bath. "Y'know," he said, "the knee feels real good."

He told Fischler that he and his friends had carried his crutches to a beach on Georgian Bay and burned them in a special ceremony. He wouldn't be needing them any more, he was sure he wouldn't. He kept telling himself that, but inside he worried.

"I hate the city," he said, steering through the beeping Toronto traffic. "Too big. Too much noise, too much traffic. C'mon, I'll show you the good life."

His sister Pat was getting married the following weekend. "Boy, do we have a lotta confusion around our house," he said.

The Ford-made car sped northward. Fischler asked Bobby about his emotions as a young hockey player. "To begin with, I'm always nervous in any game, but once I get hit, or hit somebody, it's not bad any more. In Juniors it was easy, almost like playing at home. When I came to the Bruins I was scared. I mean a lot of stuff had been written about me and I didn't know if I could play in the NHL.

"I was lucky in a way. In some training camps the rookies go here and the veterans go there. In our camp everybody was together: the rookies, the vets, the married guys and the single guys. Every one of them was just super to me."

Fischler noted that one of Bobby's favorite expressions was "super." Later he found out one reason why: it was one of the favorite expressions of almost all the Bruins.

Bobby swerved the car left at the junction of Routes 69 and 69 B. He whipped off his tie and whistled, relaxing, talking about fishing in Georgian Bay. "I just can't wait to see those bass bite," he said. "Plenty of bass, pike and pickerel, right on Georgian Bay. It's unreal!"

The car whizzed by white clapboard cottages on the edges of Parry Sound. "Be careful," Bobby yelled, laughing, as the car entered Parry Sound. "Don't blink your eyes or you'll miss it."

Fischler saw the black Parry Sound trestle and, beyond it, Georgian Bay stretching wide and blue toward the horizon. "Here ya are," Bobby yelled. "Parry Sound. Small—but she's powerful."

He parked the car near a store with a sign above it: "Ron and Bobby Orr's Clothing and Sporting Goods." Bobby's older brother, Ron, had been a slick hockey player, but he had quit. Too many people had pointed at him and said, "There's Bobby Orr's older brother." They had expected him to skate like Bobby, and no one alive could do that, so Ron gave up hockey.

After visiting his brother at the store, Bobby drove Fischler to his house. Fischler expected to see a lavish millionaire's home, maybe with a huge swimming pool and ponies in the backyard. He saw the old stucco house in which Doug Orr had raised his five children. Fischler learned that Doug Orr, earning $125 a week loading munitions in the factory, wouldn't allow Bobby to buy him a car. Arva Orr still worked part-time as a waitress in a motel coffee shop. She wouldn't allow Bobby to buy her a new house.

"They never had a great deal," Bobby said. "But they say it's *my* money. They won't take anything."

That evening Bobby introduced Fischler to two of his best friends, Neil Clairmont, a former minor league hockey player, and Bob "Homer" Holmes, whose folks owned a marina.

Bobby, his father and his friends steered a white cabin cruiser to an isolated beach a few miles from Parry Sound. From the boat they looked into a dark wilderness of pine trees. Set among the pine trees was a tiny cabin—a hideout for Bobby and his fishing pals.

Bobby pointed to bushes near the cabin. "That's where we had the crutch burning," he said laughing. "A whole bunch of people came out and burned my crutches to a crisp."

Bobby shucked off his pants and shirt. "Let's go swimming," he said laughing. Naked, he dived off the boat into the dark, cool waters of the Bay.

Pat Orr, Bobby's older sister, was now a nursing assistant. She was talking about Bobby to Toronto reporter Trent Frayne. "I can't get over how much he's matured," she said. "He used to come to me a lot to talk about things, and I often felt more than three years older. Now, I can't get over it. Even though I'm three years older, I feel I must be—oh, I don't know—a whole lot younger, I guess. He's taken it all so well, you know, and everybody's so proud. He phones home at least once a week, and everybody talks to him, all the kids and Mom and Dad. . . ."

Bobby soon could well afford those phone calls. He was earning more in one year than Doug Orr had made in 20 years. That summer (1968), with Alan Eagleson at his side, Bobby had signed a new three-year contract. The Toronto *Daily Star* reported he would get $400,000 over the three years.

Hockey finally had its first $100,000-plus player. NHL owners shuddered when they heard the news. The Boston Bruins quickly denied the story and suggested that Bobby was getting nearer $200,000 for the three years.

"I don't care if the story was wrong," said Henri Richard of the Canadiens. "It should help us all. I don't see why we can't get paid as much as the baseball and football players."

Every NHL player was saying that if Orr got a raise to more than $100,000 a year, every other player also deserved a raise.

"I think I'm half as good as Bobby Orr," said the Bruins' Eddie Westfall. "Maybe I can get half as much money."

"I hope Bobby gets one million a year," said Wayne Maki of the Black Hawks. "Every ten thousand more he gets means another thousand or two for the rest of us."

Bobby Hull demanded more money. The Hawks signed him for a reported $100,000-plus. Gordie Howe talked to the Red Wings and he signed for $80,000—the most this veteran had ever earned in 20 years of NHL service.

"I hope I can put money in everybody's pocket," Bobby said as he came to the Bruin training camp for the start of the 1968–69 season. "For that matter, I hope everyone gets twice as much as I'm getting."

When training camp opened, Bobby wasn't skating with his old speed. His knee ached. Bobby had to sit and rest for a week. Stories spread through the NHL that Orr was through.

Bobby exercised the leg in weight-lifting rooms. He came back to the ice, putting down each skate gingerly. The knee didn't hurt. As the 1968–69 season drew closer Bobby whipped himself into shape. He knew he had to be in top shape. Opposing players would be challenging him and that question mark of a knee.

It happened in the first game. The Red Wings' Howe rapped a stick across the knee. The knee held up.

A little later a linesman blew a whistle for an offside. As Bobby relaxed, Pete Stemkowski tripped him and down he went. Every eye in Boston Garden was on that knee.

Bobby got up slowly, then skated to his position, his face blank. If the knee hurt, he wouldn't let anyone see the pain. He played 25 minutes that night—and he scored the winning goal.

In the clubhouse he grinned and patted the knee. It felt good. Was he mad at Stemkowski and Howe?

He shrugged. "Listen," he said, "we all indulge in a bit of sneaky play, the little things. Those guys have a job: they have to get me. But they're good guys. In fact, you don't find many bad apples in this game."

Still, he worried all season long about the knee. He loved hockey. "You get the heck knocked out of you," he said one day to Stan Fischler, "but believe it or not, you enjoy it."

Orr and Fischler were driving up a steep hill toward Bobby's apartment overlooking Nahant Bay, some 20 miles north of Boston, where he shared an apartment with Eddie Johnston. Orr was silent a while.

"Maybe I don't show it," he said finally, "but I worry. About my health, the legs. I was worried at the start of the year that I might not be able to play. I mean, you get a little doubt and you worry. Lately I've been throwing up. The doctor says it's just nerves—I've been getting worked up too much."

"You mean they're all expecting too much from you?" Fischler asked.

"There are people who say I'm not worth that much money. You get it a lot of ways . . . I used to have a brush cut, but I let my hair grow. Now some people bug me about getting a haircut. At the games you get a few wolves here and there. But you got to take the good with the bad."

The shrieking fans, leaning over the balcony at Boston Garden, cupped their hands to their mouths to make sure their heroes got the message. Proper Bostonians didn't like their heroes with long hair in this winter of 1969. Crew cuts were still the style.

"Hey, are you a girl, Orr?" they shouted. "Then go to the beauty parlor."

Bobby brushed back his wavy blond hair as he warmed up. A few minutes later the game against the Black Hawks began.

The Hawks took a quick 1–0 lead. Then the Hawks' Pat Stapleton was sent to the penalty box, and Bobby went on the ice with four other Bruin skaters to work a "power play"—one of a number of plays used by a team to take advantage of having an extra skater.

Sanderson won the face-off—as usual. He passed to Westfall, who skated into Chicago ice. Bobby was trailing the play. Westfall dropped the puck to Bobby, and two big Black Hawks converged on him.

Bobby danced by one, shoved away the other with his left hand, then unleashed the puck from 35 feet out. It zoomed for the right corner and hit the iron backstop at the back of the net with a loud *clang!*—a sound that told the goaltender he had lost.

Five minutes later Bobby put the puck on his stick and took off on one of his rushes, coming three-quarters of the way down the ice. Black Hawks slashed at him. He dodged, twisted and sped by them all, then flipped the puck over the diving goalie and into the cage for his second goal of the night.

The fabled Eddie Shore, who played for the Bruins 40 years earlier, was one of the few defensemen in hockey history ever to achieve the three-goal "hat trick." Now some 14,000 in Boston Garden were roaring for Bobby to score one more goal.

In the second period Boston led 5–4. With Boston down a man, Chicago sent its power-play line on the ice, spearheaded by the awesome Bobby Hull and the sly Stan Mikita. Time after time Mikita and Hull drove shots at the Boston goal. Eddie Johnston stopped some, Bobby the rest—with his chest, arms and legs.

With ten minutes gone in the period, Orr rushed toward the blue line. Two defensemen began to close the gap, protecting the cage mouth. But as they did, *whap!* Bobby brought back his stick and slammed the puck on a rising line. Goaltender Dave Dryden stuck out a glove—too late. The puck was ricocheting around in the net.

The crowd stood, waves of sound thundering down on the ice. They had seen Orr perform the hat trick. Some 50 or 60 hats were sailing onto the ice. Bobby skated in small circles as teammates thumped him with their sticks. What Eddie Shore had done, young Bobby Orr had done.

Milt Schmidt watched from his seat. "You watch him every game," Milt said, "and you say, 'There's the best play he ever made.' Then you look again and he's doing something better."

A few days later Bobby was practicing at Boston Garden. First he shot left-handed, then right-handed. Only Gordie Howe could shoot with both hands. No defenseman, not even Shore, could hit both ways. Now Bobby was shooting lefty, his natural way, and teaching himself to switch and shoot righty. "Bobby never wastes a practice," said Harry Sinden.

Someone asked Bobby about the difficulties of switching. "It's like anything else," he said. "If you practice it, you'll be able to do it."

So much was being expected of him and he was barely 21. The fans wanted more goals, more assists, more victories . . . a Stanley Cup.

"I don't care how demanding they are," he said, a grim look crossing his face. "All I can do is play as well as possible. I just want to concentrate on winning this season—right up to the Stanley Cup."

Not since 1941 had any Bruin hugged the Stanley Cup. But these 1968–69 Bruins, with Bobby's knee getting stronger each week, soon roused the hopes of the loyal Bruin fans. Maybe this year . . .

Around the league teams looked at the Bruins with growing respect. "They have changed from a small meek team that often appeared to be going through the motions into a brawling, powerful unit good enough to lead the league," wrote Pete Axthelm in *Sports Illustrated*. With Teddy Green, Wayne Cashman, Ken Hodge, and Phil Esposito throwing punches, delighted fans in Boston were calling this team The Big Bad Bruins.

The Big Bad Bruins led the league for most of the season. Montreal grabbed first place only on the last weekend. Undismayed, the Bruins ran over Toronto in four straight games and took on the Canadiens in the Stanley Cup Eastern Division finals. The team that won this semi-final series would almost certainly win the Cup, since the teams in the West Division were new and weak.

In the first game the Bruins led the Canadiens with only 90 seconds left—but lost in overtime. In the second game the Bruins led with 90 seconds left—and lost again in overtime.

The Bruins bounced back. They won two straight games to even the series at two games apiece. Montreal won the next game to lead, three games to two. In the sixth game the two teams were locked in a tie in double overtime. Then Montreal's Jean Beliveau socked home a goal to win the series. A week or so later the Canadiens won the Stanley Cup.

Bobby left for home disappointed. True, he had enjoyed a marvelous year. He had knocked in 21 goals and collected 43 assists for 64 points during the season, breaking two NHL records. His 64 points and his 21 goals set new records for defensemen.

For the second straight year Bobby was the winner of the Norris Trophy as the league's outstanding defenseman. No one was even close. But as Bobby drove northward toward Parry Sound and a summer of fishing and relaxing, the tires whizzing on the road were singing a ceaseless refrain: *Stanley Cup . . . Stanley Cup . . . Stanley Cup . . .*

BIG
YEAR
FOR
BOBBY

On December 9, 1969, Bobby is receiving treatment for several minor injuries (above). But five days later he is on the ice, making a big save for the Bruins.

Bobby makes a January appearance at the All-Star banquet with superstars Esposito, Howe and Hull. In March he scores his 100th point on a goal against Detroit (bottom left) and is congratulated by his teammates.

BIG YEAR
FOR BOBBY

April is Stanley Cup playoff time. Bobby lands on the puck in front of the Bruin goal (below), gets upset by Ranger Jim Neilson (opposite), and slows down after scoring against Chicago (bottom right).

BIG YEAR FOR BOBBY

The season ends in May with smiles . . . and the Stanley Cup.

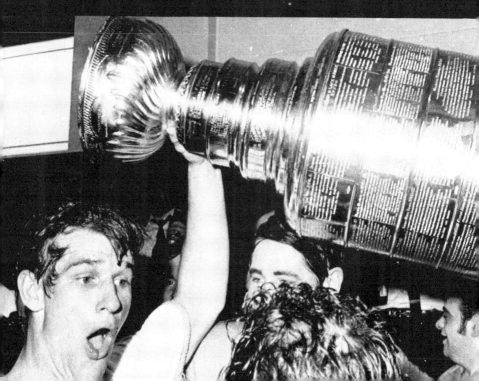

The Stanley Cup

The Bruins sat quietly in the green-carpeted clubhouse at Boston Garden. The only sounds were the tapping of sticks on stools or an occasional cough. Sweat streamed down the faces of the players in the warm room. They had just skated off the ice after their warmup drills. In a few minutes they would skate onto the ice for the fifth game of the 1969–70 Stanley Cup series against the Rangers. The two teams were tied, each having won two games in this best-of-seven series.

Halfway down the right side of the room, Bobby sat on a stool with two hockey sticks in his hands. He swung one stick, which was weighted and felt like a ton. When he swung the lighter stick in the game, it would feel as light as a feather.

Bobby gazed around the room, still swinging the weighted stick. He stood up. He walked a few feet across the room to Teddy Green's old locker.

Terrible Teddy had been severely injured in a
stick-swinging brawl earlier in the season. His
skull had been fractured and it was uncertain
whether he would ever play hockey again. Another player was sitting where Green usually sat,
but the Bruins had not forgotten their fiery leader.

Now Bobby was standing in front of Teddy
Green's replacement. Bobby tapped the man's
pads. Then he moved around the room, tapping
the pads of all the other Bruins. At 22, Bobby was
not only a star, he was becoming a leader.

"Bobby is the leader now," Gerry Cheevers told
someone later. "You watch him with the sticks
and, well, let's just say it could be pretty embar-
rassing for the guy who wasn't ready to play."

Someone said, "Let's go get 'em, gang."

The Bruins stood up and trooped out of the
room on their skates.

These 1969–70 Bruins had won 40, lost 17, and
tied 19 to finish second in the NHL East behind
Montreal. This was a goal-happy bunch that
often gave up three or four goals in a game while
knocking home six or seven of their own. Phil
Esposito, Ken Hodge, Johnny Bucyk, and other
Bruin forwards were knocking goals into the nets
at a record rate.

Yet it was not a Bruin forward who led the
league in scoring. Incredibly, it was a defenseman.
His name: Bobby Orr. For the first time in the
history of the NHL, a defenseman finished first in
scoring. "We've had a defenseman leading in
scoring after the first week of the season," said a

league official. "But never, *never* at the end of the season."

Bobby whacked 33 pucks into the nets. He had 87 assists—the most ever by *any* player, forward or defenseman. He finished with 120 points and Phil Esposito was a distant second in the league standings with 99. Bobby was only the fourth player—and the first defenseman—in league history to score more than 100 points.

Out on the ice here at Boston Garden, the Rangers brought the puck across the midline. Vic Hadfield scooted down the boards, took a pass, and shot the puck across the goal mouth.

Bobby flashed out his stick and intercepted the puck. With a push of his skates, he started up the ice. At midline he shifted into higher speed, crossed the Ranger blue line, traveling perhaps 35 miles an hour. He zipped into the gap before the Ranger defense could shut the door. He walloped the puck by goaltender Ed Giacomin and into the net. The Bruins led, 1–0.

The Rangers fought back to take the lead, 2–1. Then Esposito slammed the puck by Giacomin early in the third period to tie the game 2–2. The noisy Boston crowd nearly raised the roof.

A few minutes later Esposito—called Espy by his teammates—was circling near the Ranger blue line. Orr came up the boards with the puck shuttling on his stick.

Orr glanced at the Ranger defense. He saw the Ranger defensemen move toward him, leaving open a space between themselves and Espy. There was nothing but an expanse of ice between Espy and the Ranger goal.

Bobby nodded at Espy, who caught the sign. Bobby sped across his blue line, looking away from Espy. Espy turned, skates on the Ranger blue line. He could not cross that blue line until he got the puck; otherwise he would be offside.

Bobby, still looking one way, swatted the puck the other way—right onto Espy's stick. Like a sprinter in the 60-yard dash, Espy broke for the Ranger cage. Giacomin tensed for this one-on-one duel. The crowd let out a high-pitched shriek of anticipation. Espy drove in on Giacomin, faked a shot, then swung. The puck slammed into the cage.

Goal! The Bruins led, 3–2, and they needed no more. A few minutes later the game was over and Boston led three games to two in the series.

Two nights later the two teams met again in New York's Madison Square Garden. Ranger fans howled abuse at Bobby and Espy, trying to upset them. Bobby and Espy seemed not to hear as they warmed up, their faces expressionless.

The Rangers took an early 1–0 lead. The crowd shrieked for them to protect it, chanting "Dee-fense . . . deee-fense . . ."

Early in the second period Bobby took off on one of his rink-length dashes, swirling through the Ranger defense. He passed off the puck to Pie McKenzie, then streaked for the cage. McKenzie swatted a shot. Bobby turned and saw the puck would be wide of the cage. He reached out his stick, hooked in the puck, then slid it by Giacomin into the cage.

Goal! The game was tied 1–1.

Boston scored again to lead 2–1, a precarious lead against the Rangers and their enthusiastic fans.

The two teams swarmed up and down the ice. A Bruin intercepted a pass and knocked the puck against the right board. Bobby sprinted for the puck, high on his skates like a pirouetting ballet dancer.

He pulled the puck onto the blade of his stick, then turned and slapped the puck goal-ward. The black rubber disc zipped through a forest of padded legs. Giacomin saw the puck coming at the last moment and dove—too late. The puck rang against the iron at the back of the cage. And that sound was a funeral toll for the Rangers, behind now 3–1 with time running out.

A few minutes later the buzzer sounded, and the Bruins raised their sticks high in triumph. They had won the series and were on their way to the semi-final round against the Chicago Black Hawks.

The Rangers slouched on benches in their locker room. Their high-scoring winger, Rod Gilbert, wiped his sweat-streaked face.

"That Orr, he is impossible," he was saying to a teammate. "Hockey is a team game, right? One man is not supposed to beat a whole team, right? But what else can I say? You saw it. One man beat the Rangers in this series."

A dejected Emile Francis told newspapermen,

"Orr was the difference."

Harry Sinden laughed when he heard what Francis had said. "Orr is always the difference," he said, "because no one in hockey can match him."

Sinden told the reporters how knee trouble often hobbled Bobby. Sometimes, said Sinden, Bobby played in pain—yet he played as much as 40 minutes a game. "I know I use him a lot," the coach said with a look of remorse on his face. "But every time we're in trouble and I see him sitting on the bench, I throw him out there. I'd be crazy not to."

"Here's your dog, Mr. Orr."

"Oh, thank you."

Bobby took the dog from the small boy standing outside the front door of the house he was renting in Lynnfield, a Boston suburb. He carried the dog inside the house. The dog's name was Keoki. Sometimes Keoki strayed and the neighborhood boys returned him. On other occasions Keoki was only wandering around the backyard and he was "returned"—by boys who wanted to say hello to Bobby Orr.

Bobby set Keoki down in a corner of the living room. He had been talking to Mark Mulvoy of *Sports Illustrated*. Mulvoy asked what went on inside Bobby's head when he started out on one of those S-shaped end-to-end rushes.

"I can't explain it," Bobby said slowly. "Hockey is not that type of game. We don't have any real planned plays, like in football. I skate up

ice and look. I don't know what I'm going to do
unless it's done. You just adjust to the situation. If
the defense is split too wide, I'll try to go through.
If the defense is closed tight, I'll pass the puck. But
I never know what's going to happen until I get
there."

If Bobby didn't know what he was going to do,
then the defense was also ignorant of what he was
going to do. "Bobby changes his mind 15 or 20
times when he's skating up the ice," Derek
Sanderson told Mulvoy. "Imagine what those
defensemen must be thinking."

One night Bobby and Mark Mulvoy ate in a
Lynnfield restaurant. Within a half hour some 17
people had interrupted Bobby's dinner to ask for
his autograph. He signed for each, smiling.

Then he talked to Mulvoy about the playoffs.
"Two years ago we got into the playoffs, and
while we were congratulating ourselves, the Canadiens beat us in four straight. Last year the
Canadiens beat us in six games. I think all that is
behind us. We've been here before—and lost.
Now we're ready to win."

The organist for the restaurant came by the
table. She asked if she could play Bobby's favorite
song.

He thought for a moment. Then he smiled and
said, "Chicago."

In Chicago fans were talking excitedly about
the coming duel between the two Bobbys—Bobby
Hull against Bobby Orr. The Bruin strategy was

to try to neutralize Hull by assigning him a "shadow"—Bruin Eddie Westfall. Wherever Hull went, Westfall would follow. Westfall could cut off the puck to Hull, and without the puck, Hull couldn't unleash one of his wicked 110-mile-per-hour shots.

The Hawks could not counter with a shadow on Orr. As a defenseman, he had more room to dodge a shadow. And once Bobby got the puck, he was too fast. He would run away from any shadow.

In one game against the Black Hawks, he took off from behind the Boston cage, ducked left and then right to evade one Hawk. He dipsy-doodled by a second and simply outraced a third to roar in on the unprotected Hawk goalie—Phil Esposito's brother Tony. The luckless Tony dove onto the ice to block a shot that wasn't there, Bobby flipping the puck over him into the corner of the net for a goal.

Boston won the first three games. Hull had been unable to fire more than a half-dozen shots. In the fourth game the desperate Hawks flung the puck behind the Bruin net. They hoped to keep it in Bruin ice while looking for an open man.

"That doesn't work any more," a sad-faced Hawk coach, Billy Reay, said later. "It used to work. But now you throw it behind the Bruin cage and Bobby Orr picks it up. And there's no way you are going to take it away from him. He'll bring that puck right back to center ice as easy as you please. It didn't used to be automatic. But with Orr it's automatic."

The seemingly numbed Hawks bowed in four straight games. "Heck," said one Bruin, "most of the Hawks were just standing around and watching Bobby Orr fly, like they were in awe or something."

The Bruin fans streamed down Causeway Street, walking in the shadows of the old elevated railway, and poured into the ancient Boston Garden. They had waited since 1941 to see the Stanley Cup carried around the Garden ice by a Bruin. Now, on this sunny Sunday afternoon, May 10, 1970, the Bruins were playing the St. Louis Blues in the fourth game of the final round of the Stanley Cup playoffs. The Bruins led, three games to none. If the Bruins won this game here in Boston, before a packed house of clapping, enthusiastic fans, they would be hockey's world champions.

The Bruins burst out into a 1–0 lead. The crowd roared. St Louis jumped ahead 2–1. The crowd groaned. Espy tied the game 2–2. The crowd went wild. Early in the third period St. Louis jumped back into the lead, 3–2, and the crowd *aaaahed* its disappointment.

With some seven minutes to go, the fans were pleading for a tie that would put the game into overtime. Chief Bucyk took the puck near the boards and slapped a shot that whizzed by veteran goaltender Glenn Hall. Now the score was 3–3, and Boston Garden was a madhouse.

The clock ran out of time. As in all playoff games, there would be no tie. The first team to score in overtime would win the game. The fans in the steamy Garden stood to watch the face-off.

Facing off for the Bruins was Derek Sanderson. Again Turk won the face-off. The puck bounced to Bobby Orr, who was standing at "the point" on the blue line. Bobby saw Turk alone in the right corner. He shuttled the puck to Turk, then took off on one of those give-and-go bursts of his—sprinting right at the St. Louis cage.

In the corner Turk collected the pass and elbowed away a Blue defender. He saw Bobby rushing toward the cage. He fired the puck across the ice toward the flying Bobby.

Bobby veered between a defenseman and goaltender Hall. He reached down with the blade of his stick, stopped the puck and—in the same motion—smacked the black rubber toward the corner of the cage.

The defenseman tripped Bobby with his stick, but it was too late. As he soared high into the air—"I thought I was going to leave the rink," he said later—Bobby saw the puck bouncing in the back of the cage.

Goal! The Bruins were winners of the Stanley Cup!

A huge smile burst across Bobby's face even before he hit the ice. He thrust his stick high in triumph, then landed flat on his stomach. The Bruins, at last, were world champions.

A minute later Chief Bucyk, the oldest of the Bruins, skated around the Garden, the Stanley Cup hugged to his chest. The Boston fans roared with joy, sound seeming to pound on the ice. And as Bobby Orr came off the ice, the fans let loose a special roar.

In the sweltering clubhouse reporters ringed Orr. The winning goal had been his ninth of the playoffs. He had assisted on 11 other goals for a total of 20 points—a record in Stanley Cup playoffs for a defenseman.

"It wasn't me who scored the winning goal," he was saying, still gasping. "The credit belongs to ten bloody guys . . . the team . . . these guys I play with are unbelievable . . . just unbelievable."

It was Bobby Orr who was unbelievable—not just for what he did on the ice, but for his willingness to share the credit.

Bobby takes the daughters of teammate John McKenzie for a skate. Below, he signs autographs at a golf tournament and talks to sportswriters in the locker room.

BOBBY OFF THE ICE

"... A Genuinely Good Person"

July 4th, 1970: it was Bobby Orr Day in Parry Sound. Some 40,000 people came from Boston and from cities all over Canada to salute Bobby for what he had done during the 1969–70 season. They jammed the sidewalks to watch a parade down James Street. With the brass trumpets of oompah bands leading the way, open cars carried Derek Sanderson, Mike Walton and other hockey players here to honor Bobby. As Bobby rode by, grinning and waving, a girl dashed from the sidewalk and kissed him. Bobby reddened and people on the sidewalk laughed.

By nine that morning, lines of fans had formed outside the Kitchener Hotel to view Bobby's trophies. Thousands filed by the Hart, Ross, Norris and Smythe Trophies awarded to Bobby during his brief pro career. Also there was the Robin Hood Oats Trophy given to Bobby for being the most valuable player in some kids' tournament long forgotten. At four o'clock that afternoon people were still filing by to admire the trophies.

In the afternoon 500 people attended a luncheon honoring Bobby. Proceeds from the affair would be used to start construction in Parry Sound of the Bobby Orr Community Hockey Rink. Bobby started the fund raising by donating $1,000.

At the luncheon speakers rose to talk of Bobby. One was Father Francis Chase, a Catholic priest from a Boston suburb. Bobby sat looking down at the table as Father Chase spoke.

"Bobby is the complete hero," Father Chase told the audience. "By that I mean he's not only a great hockey player, but a great person. All he has to do is be real and not change and continue being a genuinely good person. The opportunities for a superstar to make mistakes are unlimited."

Terry Crisp, a Parry Sound boy who was now playing for the St. Louis Blues, got up. He said, "I would just like to thank the organizers of this luncheon for the opportunity to see Bobby Orr up close and standing still."

Everyone laughed and applauded. It was nice for an NHL player to see Orr at rest. Usually he was flashing by you, carrying the puck and headed for your goal.

Doug Orr spoke, saying that this day would be among the proudest moments of his life.

Then Bobby came to the microphone as the 500 people stood and applauded. Bobby began to speak. "I am sure this day will be the most memorable of my life . . ."

His throat choked and for a moment he couldn't speak. He looked out over the audience. "A man of twenty-two shouldn't have tears in his eyes," he said, and the people could see there were tears in Bobby's eyes.

After the luncheon he walked through the crowded streets of Parry Sound, fans swarming around him. He signed autographs, grinning, waving to old friends. Many were there just to get a glimpse of him. Twenty-year-old Barbara Wilson had come several hundred miles from Ottawa. "I didn't get to talk to him," she sighed, "but I saw him and I got a chance to talk to his brother Ron."

A Parry Sound resident, Mrs. Lilly Terebeyko, was walking to the drugstore when she saw Bobby emerge from a clump of autograph seekers.

"Aren't you Bobby Orr?" Mrs. Terebeyko asked.

"Yes, ma'am," Bobby said. "Say, why don't you get into the picture?"

A newspaper photographer took a picture of Bobby with his arm around the shoulder of Mrs. Terebeyko. She suddenly began to giggle.

"I hardly recognized him because his hair is longer than it used to be," she said a moment later as Bobby moved on through the admiring crowds. "Sure great to see a good boy doing so well."

As Bobby signed autographs, he talked to sportswriter Frank Orr (no relation). "People don't treat me differently here now than they ever did. It's always easy-going in Parry Sound, and nothing ever seems in a rush here. My mom thinks I don't have any private life at all, but it's not that way, really. I get lots of time to myself. Heck, the people who pay my salary, the spectators, they want to see me and talk."

Arva Orr wasn't convinced. Back in the stucco house she told a friend, "That phone never stops ringing twenty-four hours a day. Every day there are three pages of numbers for Bob to call, and a box of letters in the mail. I don't know how he ever puts up with it. His life is so hectic.

"The other day I took down all the curtains in the house to wash them. I looked out the window and three cars had stopped across the street. People were taking pictures of the house. They must have thought we were some kind of nuts, living in a house with no curtains."

Someone asked her how Bobby had changed.

"I don't think Bobby has changed much since he was a youngster, except that he seems to be a nervous wreck right now. He can't sit still for more than a minute. He's always on the go, doing something. If he and the Eagle [lawyer Alan Eagleson] were ever in the house at the same time too long, we'd have to put in one-way halls or they'd run into each other."

The Eagle was in Parry Sound at this moment. He and Bobby took care of business matters in a small office. The Eagle arranged many of Bobby's complicated business ventures, then gave him the papers to sign. Bobby signed, but he sometimes seemed more interested in whether his father had bought enough breakfast cereal for their two-day fishing trip.

"I just like to get out and relax," Bobby told a friend. "I don't get any of the big lunkers. I just like to sit out and relax . . . get out and relax where there are no telephones."

He turned to Julie, a girlfriend who was visiting from Boston. "I'm teaching her to fish," Bobby said. "She even caught a couple the other day. She's never been to a shore dinner. You know, catch the fish and cook 'em quickly right in a frying pan over a wood fire. We'll have a shore dinner tonight if I catch any fish."

That evening Bobby steered his 40-foot cabin cruiser along the edge of Georgian Bay. Tall pines stood along the shore. A cool breeze licked waves on the water. He caught a pike and later cooked it for himself, Julie and his dad. "We dip 'em in corn flakes and eggs," he told Julie, "a Canadian way of cooking 'em."

He inhaled the cool, clean air of Georgian Bay. He liked Boston. He'd never thought he would like a crowded city, but he did. Yet he would always come back to Parry Sound during the summers to fish and to laze around on his cabin cruiser, away from the ringing telephones of his hectic life.

Not that his summers were all for lazing. He taught hockey at the boys' camp he owned with Mike Walton near Toronto. They taught hockey to some 1,700 boys each summer, some of whom came from as far as California. Some of his other businesses required him to make personal appearances, too, so he was in and out of Parry Sound all the time.

Back at Parry Sound workmen were hammering together a new house for Arva and Doug Orr. People in town said it would cost $100,000. They said Bobby finally had prevailed on his parents to let him build it. All Bobby would say was, "I owe a lot to them. They raised me right."

At that moment the phone was ringing in the Orr home. Mrs. Orr picked up the receiver.

"Hello?"

"May I speak to your son?" a reporter asked.

"Which one?" asked Mrs. Orr. "I have three of them."

Alan Eagleson was talking to some writers about Bobby. "He will be a millionaire by the time he is 30," the Eagle said. "And if he isn't, I'll have done a lousy job."

"Does Orr make as much money outside of hockey as he does playing?" asked Boston writer Leo Monahan.

"Heck, yes. About three times as much," he replied. Then he listed some of the ways that Bobby made money outside hockey. He appeared in TV commercials and newspaper ads for General Motors of Canada, General Foods, Bic pens. Bobby owned a firm that made Bobby Orr hockey equipment. There were Bobby Orr hockey games. There were even Bobby Orr Pizza Parlors. He owned apartment buildings in Florida, a farm, a car wash and acres of real estate around booming Toronto.

"All of this is going on around him," Eagleson said, "and he doesn't give a darn. He gave me a check last June that he's had in his wallet since January 18th. It was for $11,000. I think one reason for this is that a part of him doesn't want to have this kind of money because it sets him apart from his teammates."

"He's a bleeding heart and a do-gooder, that's all," Eagleson told Jack Olsen of *Sports Illustrated*. There was a note of exasperation in the Eagle's voice. "And most of it is private. He won't even tell me about it. He doesn't get receipts and we lose all kinds of tax deductions because he doesn't make a record of it. Every once in a while he cleans out his whole wardrobe and gives it to the priest over at the Sacred Heart in Watertown. No, Bobby's not Catholic . . . but he's the most Christian man I've ever known.

"He'll get $500 for an appearance somewhere, and he'll give it to the first charity worker he sees. I asked him what happened to his bonus check last year. He says, 'Oh, I remember. I endorsed it over to Father Chase.'

"You wouldn't have space to list the things he's honorary chairman of: Muscular Dystrophy Association of Canada, United Fund of Boston, March of Dimes, all kinds of things. But that isn't where his time goes. His time goes in visiting hospitals, orphan homes, poor kids, things like that. It's more than a duty with him, it's an obsession."

They wheeled the children into Bobby's apartment. They were children crippled by cerebral palsy. From their wheelchairs they smiled at Bobby. A photographer came in after them. He asked Bobby to stand behind the wheelchairs. He snapped a photo of Bobby with the kids. The picture would be used to help raise money for cerebral palsy research.

The photographer left. "Let's go, Bobby," yelled John "Frosty" Foristall, his roommate, who is the assistant Bruin trainer. "We'll be late for the game."

"That's all right, we have time," Bobby said. And for some 20 minutes he hunched over the wheelchairs and chatted with these kids about hockey.

For a week writer Jack Olsen tried to dig out of Bobby why he did so much for charity. Bobby would change the subject. But one day, sitting in a Boston restaurant, Bobby turned to Olsen and said, "OK, I'm lucky, right? I've been gifted, right? But the world is full of people who've not been gifted. Not only haven't they been gifted, but they have had things taken away from them. All I have to do is see one of them—some little girl that can't walk and yet she keeps on smiling at me, some lady like Deanna Deleidi who goes home to an iron lung every night and still gives me a kiss and a hug after every hockey game.

"All I have to do is see someone like that and then I don't think I'm such a big hero any more. I think that compared to those people I'm a very small article! A very small, lucky article! It knocks me down pretty bloody fast. It cuts deep into me, and I'd rather not talk about it. It's very personal with me."

A Bruin fan, Tom Capucci, came out of the Boston Garden after a game and walked down Causeway Street to the parking lot. He pulled his overcoat collar around him. Sleet bit into his face, an icy wind made him shiver.

He started his car and stepped on the gas. The car skidded on ice. Tom gunned the engine. The car bucked but wouldn't budge, its rear tires spinning on the ice.

Another motorist got out of his car and came over. He got behind Tom's car. "You steer," he hollered, "and I'll push."

The sleet was drenching the pusher. But he kept on pushing. Some 20 minutes later Tom's car skidded free of the ice.

Tom rolled down his window. "Thanks," he hollered out into the wind and sleet.

"That's OK," the stranger shouted back, and it was only then that Tom saw who it was: Bobby Orr.

A writer, Stan Fischler, mentioned the incident months later to Bobby. "What the heck?" said Bobby, a little embarrassed. "He would have done the same for me."

I dined one night with Phil Esposito and his wife in a restaurant near the Boston Garden. I was interviewing Esposito for a *Sport* magazine story.

"Let's go over to Bobby's place," he said, "he's having a party."

"Would it be all right if I came?" I asked.

"Sure," Espy said, but I felt uncomfortable. No one likes to be the uninvited guest.

We drove to Orr's high-rise apartment in midtown Boston. Espy parked the car in the apartment's underground garage. An elevator took us some 20 floors high. We pressed the buzzer. Orr opened the door.

He was dressed casually. "Hi, John," he said, reaching out to shake my hand. I felt flattered. He had remembered my name even though we had met only once or twice before.

"Come on in, make yourselves comfortable," he told us. Other players were here with their wives or girlfriends: Eddie Johnston, Don Marcotte, Derek Sanderson.

We sat on chairs or couches. Bobby served cold drinks, pretzels, peanuts, small sandwiches. "Everybody have enough?" he kept asking. He was obviously concerned that everyone was having a good time.

He told a joke on himself. At a party in honor of Britain's Prince Charles, the Prince knew most everyone at the party. But when Bobby was introduced, the Prince said, "And Mr. Orr, what is it that you do?"

Bobby laughed, obviously amused at this put-down of himself.

The party ended near midnight. As we left,

IS NUMBER   1.

Bobby helped some of us put on our coats. He gripped my hand. "I hope you had a good time," he said. "Come again. It was a pleasure having you."

"That's the way he is to everyone," Phil Esposito said afterward. "The Bobby Orr you saw tonight, that's the real Bobby Orr."

One of Bobby's friends is Pat Considine, a longshoreman on the Boston docks. Pat got to know the Bruins by eating in the places around Boston Garden where the players eat. He knows all of them—especially Eddie Johnston and Bobby.

On weekends and summer evenings Pat plays softball with his neighborhood team. Each year there is a dinner for the softball team at an American Legion Hall in Pat's neighborhood. One year Pat invited Bobby to come.

Bobby came, sat in a corner and talked sports with Pat and his softball-playing friends for four or five hours.

"Hey, I had a great time," Bobby told Pat when the evening had ended. "Would you invite me next year?"

Pat did invite Bobby the next year. And Bobby came.

Ray Reid sat in the Parry Sound bus station. He was nervous. He was leaving Parry Sound to go to Kitchener and try out with the Kitchener Rangers in the Ontario Hockey Association Junior A League. He hoped to make the team. He had been playing on defense for the Parry Sound Junior C team.

Ray looked up and saw Bobby Orr, who was saying goodbye to a friend who was leaving on the same bus. "I'm goin' to take a shot with the big fellas," Ray told Bobby.

Bobby left his friend and walked with Ray to a corner of the station. He gave Ray some tips on playing defense in Junior A.

Later Ray was talking on the bus with Bobby's friend. "It's a funny thing," Ray said. "I went to a hockey school a few weeks ago, and they had this big guy from the NHL. He could hardly make the team, but he acted like he was the greatest. And here's Bobby, who *is* the greatest, and he thinks nothing of helping me when he can."

"Hey, how much did you pay for that shirt?" Orr shouts at his roommate, Frosty Foristall, in the Bruin locker room.

"Thirteen dollars, I think."

"For that price you coulda got a new one!" Orr yells, and bursts out laughing.

When the other players arrive, Bobby sees Turk Sanderson. "Turk's been calling me Slippery Lips ever since we had a big argument the other night," Bobby tells Jack Olsen. "He said that in football a field goal's measured from the line of scrimmage, and I said it's measured from the point of the kick. I proved it to him, but he still won't admit I'm right. Watch!"

Bobby shouts down the long clubhouse, "Hey, Turk, a field goal's measured from the point of the kick, right?"

"No!" Turk shouts back.

A little later the Bruins start out for the game. As Sanderson passes Orr he says, "It's measured from the line of scrimmage!"

"OK, OK," Orr says, grinning, "if you say so, Turk." And together they go out to play hockey.

THE ALL-ROUND PLAYER

Amazing Bobby clears the puck from in front of the Bruin goal. . .

. . . fights for the puck at mid-ice (left), drives on the enemy goal (center), fights his way through a pack of enemy defenders (right), and shoots (below).

The Genius of Orr

Each year the National Hockey League awards seven major trophies:

- The Calder Memorial Trophy to the rookie of the year.
- The Vezina Trophy to the goalkeepers who yield the fewest goals.
- The Lady Byng Memorial Trophy to the player judged most gentlemanly—in the sense that he spends least time in the penalty box.
- The Art Ross Trophy to the player who leads the league in scoring.
- The James Norris Memorial Trophy to the best defenseman in the league.
- The Hart Memorial Trophy to the player judged most valuable to his team.
- And the Conn Smythe Trophy to the player judged most valuable to his team in the Stanley Cup playoffs.

In the 1969–70 season, Bobby Orr was not eligible for the Calder Trophy because he was not a rookie. He was not eligible for the Vezina Trophy because he was not a goalie—although his teammates said he made almost as many saves as the goalkeepers.

Bobby did not win the Lady Byng. St. Louis' Phil Goyette took it for having spent only 16 minutes in the penalty box during the entire season. Bobby, playing with the rougher Bruins, spent 91 minutes in the box.

But in that 1969–70 season Bobby captured all the other trophies. He won the Ross Trophy as the league's highest scorer with 33 goals and 87 assists for 120 points—the first defenseman ever to win the award.

He won the Norris Trophy as the league's best defenseman—for the third straight season. Indeed the Rangers' Harry Howell now seemed a prophet for saying, after winning the Norris in 1967: "I'm glad I won it this year because Bobby Orr is going to win it for the next ten years."

Bobby won the Hart Trophy as the league's Most Valuable Player. And finally, he won the Conn Smythe Trophy as the outstanding player in the playoffs—his 20 points a playoff record for a defenseman.

Yet, despite all those awards that Orr had won, new hockey fans often asked, Why was Bobby Orr rated so highly? He skated with eye-catching grace. But to a casual observer Orr didn't seem all that outstanding.

You had to watch him play for a stretch of time—and then talk to the hockey veterans who played with him and against him—to fully grasp what hockey coaches often termed "the genius of Orr."

The Bruins, playing St. Louis, are one man short because of a penalty. There are 30 seconds left in the penalty as St. Louis organizes a charge, five Blues skaters whirling around the Boston cage like Indians around a wagon train.

Christian Bordeleau cranks up to shoot. Bobby Orr skims right at him, kneeling, and sweeps his stick across the ice. The sweep bats away the puck, but the stick is knocked out of Bobby's hand.

He sees the puck bouncing onto the stick of another Blues skater, who winds up to shoot. Bobby skates without a stick right into the path of the puck and kicks it away with his skate.

He chases after the puck, still stickless, knocks aside one Blues skater and freezes the puck with his skate against the boards.

"Did you ever see a hockey player do things like that?" asks the Bruin coach after the game. And back comes the reply: "No, never."

During one stretch of time in the 1967–68 season, the Bruins won 22 games, lost 12 and tied 7 with Bobby on ice. Then he was out for almost a month. During that period the Bruins were 10-10-3. "Without Orr," said Alan Eagleson, Bobby's attorney, "the Bruins are a .500 hockey team. With him they are a .700 club."

"Bobby Orr and Phil Esposito run the Bruin offense," Bobby Hull told Chris Lydon of *Sport* magazine one day. "Orr, I would say, creates the situation. Esposito puts the puck away. They both know that when one of them has the puck, something is going to happen. Esposito gets it done in our end. Orr gets it done in both ends. If Orr isn't going, they're not the same club."

Bobby intercepts a pass some 20 feet in front of the mouth of the Minnesota cage. Goalkeeper Cesare Maniago bends his knees and tenses, expecting the shot.

Bobby winds up and swings, but aims the puck at Phil Esposito near the corner of the cage. Espy drills it by the startled Maniago.

"Bobby always works like that," Espy says later. "He's always thinking about the team. Even I thought he should have taken that shot."

"The guys tell me I'd better hurry up if I'm going to catch up with Bobby Orr, but they all know I'll never catch up," defenseman Brad Park of the Rangers was saying. "He can skate circles around J. C. Tremblay and he can skate circles around me. His most effective thing is his skating. Because of his speed, he's always got that extra split second to do something extra with the puck. When somebody moves to the outside around Bobby, he'll take three steps toward him and just snatch the puck away from him. I'd have to take a guy into the corner and try to tie him up. Bobby moves a guy to the outside where he knows he can catch him."

Orr scores a goal on a power play to tie the Philadelphia Flyers, 2–2. A minute later the Flyers' Jim

Johnson bursts loose near center ice and streaks on a solo flight toward the Bruin goalie. Bobby turns, speeds after Johnson, catches him and knocks the puck away.

A little later the Bruins are a man short. Bobby steals the puck from a Flyer shooter and starts up ice. Three Flyers pursue him. Suddenly he stops, the Flyers zooming by him. The crowd laughs and applauds.

The three Flyers skid to a stop, turn and come back. Bobby skates in a lazy circle until two Flyers are almost on top of him. He suddenly takes off, still cradling the puck. He skims along the boards, dodges one Flyer, then another, crosses the Flyers' blue line and bears down on goalie Doug Favell. He shoots. Favell blocks the shot, and someone freezes the puck.

There is a face-off. The puck is shuttled toward Bobby at the blue line. He winds up and blasts a shot by Favell that wins the game, 3–2.

"There are a few little things that the public doesn't know about Bobby," said the Rangers' Glen Sather. "He never wears socks under his skates. He says he skates better without socks. I've seen three phases in his career: the first year or so when he was learning, and frustrated, when he got hit a lot. There was a second phase when nobody on his team knew what to do with him. And now a third phase when everybody is beginning to understand him and he's starting to play with the rest of his team, letting the others do a lot of the work but still controlling the game."

Rosaire Paiement of the Canucks checks Bobby, then knocks him to the ice with his elbow. Bobby jumps up and charges at Paiement.

Paiement is a good fighter. He ducks a punch and throws a right, cutting Bobby above the eye. Officials break up the fight. In the third period Orr charges Paiement and throws another punch. Paiement hits him again in the eye.

"He's proud," Paiement said later. "He is a good fighter. But fighting is sort of my game. Why in the world should he be rough? He's got all the ability in the world. The kid's got everything."

"You say about each of the great players: he's a good skater, or a particularly good stick-handler, or he has a great shot, but something is always missing," veteran goalie Jacques Plante once told Chris Lydon. "Bobby Orr has it all. He is the best I've seen—ever. He does everything right. In front of his own net every other defenseman will have a blind side, or will miss something that's developing behind him. But Bobby Orr is unreal, he sees everything. He's got a mean streak, which makes him a lot better. Doug Harvey was the same way. When he hits you, he hits you harder than you expect.

"He can shoot from 40 feet and his shot is always on the net—that is very important. He can also move in close. When he comes in on the outside he reaches a point near the goal where the angle is against him and most players would pass. Now, say Esposito is waiting on the other side of the net. I can't turn and play the pass because Bobby Orr has the strength to shoot even when the angle is bad—or to bull his way in front of the net and shoot from there."

Bobby skims along the ice, does that one-two twirling dance of his, circles around Stan Mikita and bears down on Black Hawk defensemen Bill White and Paul Smyre.

The Hawk defensemen converge so Bobby can't get between them. Bobby slides a lateral pass to Fred Stanfield, coming down on a wing. The defense now splits, White moving over to cover Stanfield. Orr slides through the hole in the defense, takes the return pass from Stanfield, and faces goaltender Tony Esposito, who has no chance, no chance at all. Another goal for Bobby Orr.

"Most wings come down on you at one speed and then turn on a burst," said defenseman Bob Plager. "But Orr can break into a third speed and then turn into a fourth. You just can't keep up with him . . ."

"That pivot of his," said another defenseman, Bill White. "It's what makes him so hard to check. He has terrific balance. He comes at you, stops, pivots and starts so quickly he's around you while you've just come to a stop."

"I've never seen a player change gears like him," said ex-forward Vic Stasiuk. "He must have at least six different gears. He just slows down a bit, then goes into another gear and he's by you. Orr is unreal. They ought to have one league for him and another for the rest of us."

"I knew he was going to be a superstar," said Ranger coach Emile Francis. "I knew it when he was only coming along. But I never thought it would be this early. At 27, yes. But he's only in his early 20s and he's the greatest performer in the game, ever. They say a defenseman doesn't come into his prime until he is 27 or 28. What is Bobby Orr going to be like when he is 27 or 28? They'll have to take his skates away from him and make him play against the rest of us in his bare feet. And he'd still be great."

UPS AND DOWNS

UPS AND DOWNS

Bruin sticks go up in triumph when a goal is scored in 1973. The Bruins lost the Cup, but Bobby remained the most popular star in the game.

The
Extra
Man

Bobby and the Bruins skated onto the ice at Madison Square Garden for this sixth game of the 1971–72 Stanley Cup finals. The Bruins led the Rangers in this final round, three games to one. Win this game and the Bruins would be Stanley Cup champions for the second time in three years. But they couldn't take that Cup for granted. No, sir. Look what had happened a year earlier.

In 1970–71 the Bruins had won the Prince of Wales Trophy by finishing first in the NHL East. The team had been a powerhouse, racking up more than a dozen NHL scoring records. Bobby had finished second in league scoring behind Espy and set new scoring records for a defenseman with 37 goals and 102 assists. He became the first player in NHL history to score 100 or more points two seasons in a row. No one ever had done that—not Beliveau, Howe or Hull. Bobby won the Norris Trophy as the league's best defenseman for the fourth straight time. He won the Hart

Trophy as the league's most valuable player for the second year in a row.

Then what happened? Then these proud Bruins, the highest-scoring team in hockey history, skated into the first round of the Stanley Cup playoffs against the Montreal Canadiens—and lost, four games to three.

What had gone wrong? Montreal's Henri Richard summed it up this way: "In the last two games we shadowed Orr with a leftwinger. We checked him, we tired him out. That had to help us because Orr is 40 percent of their team."

"The Bruins will come back," Bobby said in the summer of 1971. And he was right—the 1971–72 Bruins had come back.

They won the Prince of Wales Trophy for the second straight season by finishing first in the NHL East. Again Bobby finished second in the league in scoring behind Espy. He scored 37 goals and 80 assists for 117 points—the third straight year he had scored more than 100. For the fifth straight season—another record—he won the Norris Trophy as the league's best defenseman. For the third straight season—yes, *another* record —he won the Hart Trophy as the league's Most Valuable Player.

But now, warming up for this sixth game of the final round of the 1971–72 Stanley Cup playoffs, Bobby knew the season would be a flop for the Bruins if they didn't win the Cup.

If only his knee was all right. That left knee, the one he had injured in a charity game years ago, pained him. Doctors had looked at the knee and found floating cartilage. Another operation was needed as soon as the season was over.

In the fifth game, Bobby had led the Bruins to a 3–2 victory, scoring two goals and an assist. Now, if only the knee would hold up for one more game, the season would be over.

The pain made him wince. Ice bags were strapped to the knee. Sometimes the knee locked. He would try to turn on the ice, and it would lock. Doctors injected painkillers into the knee, but the pain throbbed anyway. During this game, he would have to hobble off the ice every 15 minutes to get fresh ice packs.

The game began. Bobby skated doggedly up and down the ice, trying to forget the pain. Midway through the period the Bruins threw the puck behind the Ranger net and swarmed in after it. Bobby skated to "the point" on the blue line.

The puck slithered out toward him and Ranger Bruce McGregor chased after it. Bobby arrived at the puck a second ahead of McGregor. The safe play was to whack the puck against the nearby boards. Instead Bobby thrust the puck right into McGregor's path, like casting bait to a fish. McGregor lunged for the puck. If he grabbed it, he would have a straight, open run at the Bruin goal.

Bobby swiped the puck back onto his stick. He twirled on that bad knee and suddenly he was around McGregor and had a clear shot at the Ranger goal. Back came the Orr stick—*whack!*

The puck flew through a tangle of legs and slid under goaltender Gilles Villemure's pads. *Goal!* Boston led, 1–0.

The Bruins still held that slender lead when midway through that period the Bruins lost two men to the penalty box. Now they had only three skaters on the ice to defend against five Ranger skaters. Some 17,000 Ranger fans in Madison Square Garden were screaming for a score.

Bobby skated on to defend against the Ranger power play. On the face-off he grabbed the puck and seemed to glue it to his stick. For long stretches of the penalty time the Rangers could not knock the puck off that magic stick. Bobby cruised around the ice, killing time until the Bruins again had all five skaters on ice.

The Bruins still led 1–0 early in the third period. Bobby took a face-off pass from Esposito, cruised past the blue line and whizzed a shot at Villemure. The puck slanted off Wayne Cashman's stick and flew into the cage. An assist for Bobby, a goal for Cashman and the Bruins led 2–0.

That goal seemed to deflate the Rangers. Boston scored again, and minutes later the buzzer sounded. The Bruins were Stanley Cup champions. The fans applauded as Chief Bucyk skated around the rink clasping the Stanley Cup.

In the Ranger dressing room Vic Hadfield looked back on the series between the two hard-hitting teams. "The two clubs were even in face-offs," he said, "even in power plays, even in penalty killings, even in everything—except they had Bobby Orr."

Up in the press box Stan Fischler was writing a report on the playoffs for the *Sporting News*. He noted that Esposito had failed to score a goal in the final five games of the series. "Esposito's failure," Fischler wrote, "underlined the point that the Bruins can win without production from their leading scorer, but they cannot win without Orr."

In the clubhouse a grinning Orr held the Cup and drank champagne from it. He had been named the winner of the Conn Smythe Trophy as the playoffs' Most Valuable Player—his second Smythe in three years. He had won three straight Hart Trophies, five straight Norris Trophies.

He had them all—plus a left knee that throbbed with pain. Brittle Bob. Maybe this time he really was finished.

In June doctors cut open the knee and tightened the ligaments. He was now one of the world's richest patients. A few weeks earlier he had signed a contract with the Bruins for one million dollars to be paid over the next five years. He was one of the world's highest-paid athletes. But if he couldn't play, he wasn't going to get paid anything.

"This operation is your only hope," doctors told him. "You couldn't go on playing the way your knee was."

"I know," Bobby said. "I played for a long time when the knee was sore and it was unbearable. I couldn't play the game the way I wanted. In fact, I could hardly play at all."

All summer long he exercised the knee. He hoped he would be able to play for Team Canada, a team of NHL All-Stars that would oppose the Russian National Team. Team Canada flew to Sweden to practice. Walking down a street Bobby suddenly stumbled and almost fell. The knee had locked.

Was he through? If he couldn't walk down a street how could he play hockey?

He watched on a TV set in a Moscow hotel room as Team Canada edged out the Russian team in close contests. He couldn't play, the knee hurt so much. And he couldn't bear to watch the games in an arena—he wanted too badly to skate out there on the ice.

He tried to play at the start of the 1972–73 season but the knee still ached. "Quit for three weeks," a doctor told him. "Concentrate on building up the leg and the knee."

Bobby skated 90 minutes a day in the Boston Garden. He rode an exercise bike for five miles, for ten miles. He worried.

November 18, 1972: Bobby skated onto the ice to play the Islanders in New York, his first appearance since his layoff. He saw the puck skid toward him. Back went his stick—his first shot of the night, his first shot in three weeks. *Whack! Goal!* Just like that, on his first shot, Bobby had scored.

A little later he tried to veer around Jim Mair. The Islander hip-checked Bobby, catching him on that vulnerable left knee. Bobby was flipped high into the air and came down on the ice with a thump.

He jumped up, angry and not thinking about the knee. He skated after the puck. The knee was all right. It didn't buckle. Bobby Orr seemed like the old Bobby Orr.

Without Orr the Bruins had been playing .500 hockey. In the six weeks after his return the Bruins won 14 games, lost only one, and soared from third to first in the NHL East. On New Year's Day, 1973, Bobby celebrated by collecting six assists, tying a record for defensemen, to help beat the Vancouver Canucks, 8–2. First-place Boston now led Montreal by two points.

In only 25 games Bobby had scored 11 goals and had 30 assists for 41 points. He was ranked among the league's top 25 scorers—even though he had missed 14 games. Despite his late start he lagged only eight assists behind the two leaders, Stan Mikita and Gil Perreault. At the rate he was racking up assists, he seemed likely to lead the league in assists for the fourth straight season. His contributions were particularly welcome since two of the stars of the Bruin Stanley Cup team—Turk Sanderson and Gerry Cheevers—had jumped to the World Hockey Association. The Bruins needed Bobby more than ever.

Then, suddenly, Bobby wasn't skating with his usual verve. Immediately the Bruins slumped, losing five of eight games and dropping out of first place.

HOCKEY'S BIG QUESTION: WHAT'S WRONG WITH ORR?

That New York *Post* headline early in February 1973, introduced a story that told of the Bruins' slump and Bobby's problems. In a game in New York against the Rangers Bobby slipped three times on the ice.

After three operations on his left knee in five years, wrote Hugh Delano, "Orr . . . seemed to be favoring his surgically repaired knee. He didn't rush or skate as usual last night. He didn't look like the Bobby Orr of old."

It was only a slump, Bobby insisted. "I've just had two left feet lately," he was telling people with a grin. "I'll be all right."

He proved he was all right. He proved he was still the same dazzling Bobby Orr just a few games later when he scored one goal and assisted on three others to beat the Toronto Maple Leafs. Now there could be little doubt: Bobby Orr was back and he was as great as ever.

Bobby finished third in the league in scoring in 1972–73 with 29 goals and 72 assists for a total of 101 points. He was far behind the leaders in goals and was second behind Esposito in assists. Yet Bobby became the first player ever to score 100 or more points four seasons in a row. And Bobby had accomplished this feat while missing more than a month of play. It had not been a great season either for him or for the Bruins, but most hockey players would give plenty to have one season as good.

In his apartment 20 floors above midtown Boston, Bobby was boiling shrimp for lunch and talking to a guest, Mark Mulvoy of *Sports Illustrated.*

"I'm a smarter player now," Bobby said. He and Mulvoy had been discussing the 1972–73 season under new coach Bep Guidolin who had been Bobby's coach with the Oshawa Generals. "Or at least I think I am . . . I have found out that you can save a lot of energy by being smart on the ice, by passing the puck more. Why crack through two defensemen yourself when you can pass the puck to a teammate, then sneak around behind the defenseman and get a return pass? Also, why go between a guy and the boards when the odds are that you won't make it? I'm just learning those things."

In the 1973 Stanley Cup playoffs, the Bruins faced their old rivals, the New York Rangers, in the first round. Nothing went right for Boston and New York eliminated Orr's Bruins in only five games.

When the final buzzer sounded, the Rangers lined up to shake hands with the Bruins, a tradition in all playoff final games. Some Bruins, angered and humiliated by their defeat, hurried off the ice. But Bobby Orr stayed, leading a parade of Bruins down the line of Rangers. Bobby made a special point to congratulate Ranger goalie Ed Giacomin, who had been one of the heroes of the series.

As Orr skated off toward the locker room, Ranger telecaster Bill Chadwick said, "There goes Bobby Orr—a real sportsman and probably the greatest hockey player who ever lived."

Bob Feller began pitching for baseball's Cleveland Indians when he was 17 years old. Johnny Bench became an All-Star catcher at 20. Kareem Abdul-Jabbar emerged to dominate pro basketball in his early 20s, and football's Joe Namath was a star at the same age.

But no one in any sport captured the imagination (or the awards) at so early an age as Bobby Orr. As the 1973 season approached its conclusion, Bobby turned 25. He was completing his seventh full season with the Bruins, and if he never played another game, his name would be remembered forever in pro hockey.

With good fortune, Bobby's career had only begun. As Emile Francis had said, defensemen seldom reach their peak until their late 20s. And some have played until they were nearly 40. So the Bobby Orr story is far from finished, and already it is one of the most amazing in all sport.

For the Bruins, Bobby is more than a star. Brad Park, often called "the second-best defenseman in hockey," put it best when he said, "When Bobby's on the ice, you're playing against an extra man."

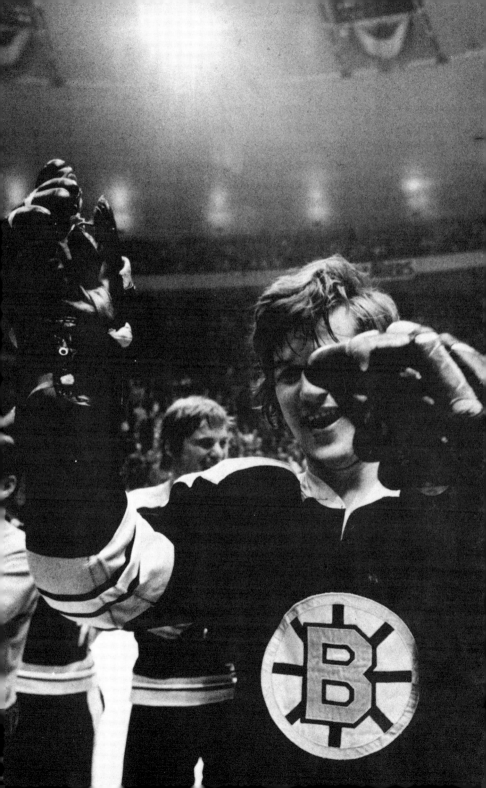

INDEX